Gifted Bilingual Students

RETHINKING CHILDHOOD

Joe L. Kincheloe and Janice A. Jipson
General Editors

Vol. 17

PETER LANG
New York • Washington, D.C./Baltimore • Bern
Frankfurt am Main • Berlin • Brussels • Vienna • Oxford

Esther Kogan

Gifted Bilingual Students

A Paradox?

PETER LANG
New York • Washington, D.C./Baltimore • Bern
Frankfurt am Main • Berlin • Brussels • Vienna • Oxford

Library of Congress Cataloging-in-Publication Data

Kogan, Esther.
Gifted bilingual students: a paradox? / Esther Kogan.
p. cm. — (Rethinking childhood; vol. 17)
Includes bibliographical references.
1. Linguistic minorities—Education—United States. 2. Education, Bilingual—United
States. 3. Gifted children—United States—Identification. I. Title. II. Series.
LC3731 .K64 371.95'2—dc21   00-037530
ISBN 0-8204-5016-2
ISSN 1086-7155

Die Deutsche Bibliothek-CIP-Einheitsaufnahme

Kogan, Esther:
Gifted bilingual students: a paradox? / Esther Kogan.
—New York; Washington, D.C./Baltimore; Bern;
Frankfurt am Main; Berlin; Brussels; Vienna; Oxford: Lang.
(Rethinking childhood; Vol. 17)
0-8204-5016-2

Cover design by Lisa Dillon

The paper in this book meets the guidelines for permanence and durability
of the Committee on Production Guidelines for Book Longevity
of the Council of Library Resources.

Printed in the United States of America

To my parents with endless love and admiration

꧁꧂

Table of Contents

Acknowledgments

As with any complex endeavor, this book is the result of the support, encouragement, and guidance of a number of mentors, colleagues, friends, and loved ones over the past several years. The results of their efforts, suggestions, and patience are reflected in every page of this book. It is with great pleasure that I take this opportunity to acknowledge and thank those people.

To Dr. James Borland, my sponsor and professor at Teachers College, Columbia University, for all his support throughout the course of my graduate studies. His direction and expert guidance facilitated the completion of the original document; Dr. Olga Rubio, for all her courteous suggestions that clarified and enhanced this study in its initial steps; Dr. Lisa Wright, for all her prudent advisements throughout my educational career, and her continuous support, insights, and encouragement.

I wish to thank Connie Coulianos, my dearest friend and colleague, with whom over the years I discussed, listened to, shared, and affirmed ideas that enriched my professional life.

To my dear friend Deby Benchoam from whom I learned that no matter how harsh life is upon us, we can still have a smile on our face.

I am forever grateful to the three wonderful students and their mothers for enabling this study to take place. Their experiences, perspectives, and thoughts were always interesting and inspiring. The mothers' dedication and advocacy to give their children the best educational opportunities possible demonstrates their commitment to enhancing their children's lives.

There are other debts as well, intensely personal and closer to home. To my dear Ruben, my friend and companion, who has enriched and brightened my days. Also to my beautiful children, Tanya and Itamar, for making me laugh, and for making me the proudest *mama*. I hope I can communicate as much love as I feel for the three of them.

To all my beloved family and friends I give loud, proud, and deepest thanks. Their faith in my educational endeavors has been a constant source of strength and motivation.

Lastly, I would like to thank my parents, who mediated the world for me and thus facilitated the development of an intrinsic framework that enabled me to be who I am. To my late *chula*, for her part in instilling in me confidence, endurance, and kindness. I missed you. To my *pa,* for his part in teaching me the understanding of values, respect, and faith.

Esther Kogan
New York

Part I

---

*Bilingual Education
in the United States*

꧁꧂

Chapter One

Historical Background of Bilingual Education in the United States

Large numbers of people speaking languages other than English migrated to this country in the nineteenth and twentieth centuries. The massive wave of immigration was triggered by the American asylum and refugee policies. The overall direction of new policies was toward greater universalism, eliminating previous discriminatory racial barriers and opening the doors of the country on the basis of uniform criteria. Since 1965, occupational skills, family reunification, and fear of political persecution have been the guiding criteria of U.S. immigration policy (Portes & Schauffler, 1996).

But despite the volume of the immigration population, the federal government paid little attention to bilingual education or to the problems of non-English-dominant minority students until 1968, when President Lyndon B. Johnson signed the Bilingual Education Act into law. Prior to 1968, no programs of bilingual-bicultural education existed at the federal level. Virtually all educational arrangements were a matter of state and local initiatives that varied considerably from place to place.

The motivations behind the enactment of the Bilingual Education Act (Title VII of the Elementary and Secondary Education Act) in 1968 were twofold. First, the size of the non-English-speaking population in many parts of the country was growing and showed no signs of any future decrease. Second, education was becoming much more important in terms of employment and social mobility than in previous generations, and it was becoming clear to some that equal educational opportunity was a myth for large numbers of students not able to learn in English. Second-language-learner students, particularly Hispanics, were seriously disadvantaged educationally; their dropout rate was high, and they fell behind their peers in content area learning. The Civil Rights movement of the sixties, which raised the concept of equal-educational opportunities, had raised the consciousness of the nation about discrimination against African-Americans, and this concern was transferred to language minorities as well. Indeed, the Civil Rights Act of 1964 itself became the chief impetus for bilingual education in the United States.

However, bilingual education in the early 1960s was seen as a remedial/compensatory approach to the education of second-language-speaking children. Students who spoke a language other than English were considered "culturally disadvantaged" and in need of compensatory education that would compensate for those handicaps. More specifically, in 1967, when the United States Senate held the first congressional hearing ever on the subject of bilingual education, the legislators proposed the use of bilingual instruction as a transition from the use of the native language in informal situations to the exclusive use of English in the formal setting of the schools. This linguistic assimilation was part of a more comprehensive and highly desirable cultural assimilation. So bilingual education was seen only as an educational strategy designed to remediate the effects of cultural disadvantagedness.

When the Bilingual Education Act (BEA) was adopted in 1968, a new educational age began. The BEA became part of a process of formulating status and planning goals concerning the future of bilingual education in the United States. This act was the first categorical federal law authorizing bilingual-bicultural educational programs.

The act recognized the rights of children with limited English ability to learn about their cultural heritage and to be taught in their native language. In sum, the Bilingual Education Act of 1968 was intended as a demonstration program designed to meet the educational needs of low-income, limited English-speaking children. Several outcomes came out of this initiative: Grants were awarded to local educational agencies, institutions of higher education, or regional research facilities to develop and operate bilingual educational programs, native history and culture programs, early childhood education programs, adult education programs, and programs to train bilingual aides. Efforts were made to attract and retain as teachers individuals from non-English-speaking background; and efforts were made to establish cooperation between the home and the school (August & Garcia, 1988).

The Bilingual Education Act has been reauthorized on five occasions (1974, 1978, 1984, 1988, and 1993). The several amendments provided an opportunity and an obligation to develop new national educational policies and programs that could respond to the current realities of this country. In other words, the trend went from defining a bilingual education program for the first time as instruction given in English to the extent necessary to allow a child to progress effectively through the education system; to the clarification of the definition of eligible children as "Limited-English-Proficient" (LEP); to the development of a wide variety of bilingual programs and provisions that support the needs of special populations such as bilingual preschool-age children, special education groups, and gifted and talented students; and finally to the allocation of funds for research, evaluation, training, and dissemination initiatives (Aleman, 1993; August & Garcia, 1988).

All major reauthorizations of the BEA of 1968 were strongly influenced and defined by several federal cases that have been an avenue of educational programs for second-language-learner students. The major court decision on the rights of second-language-learner students, and the only such ruling by the U.S. Supreme Court, is *Lau* v. *Nichols* (1974). It was initiated in California and involved a claim by a group of Chinese parents who complained that when their children attended classes with mainstream students, their inability to understand English instruction prevented them from receiving an equal education. Bilingual education, specifically, was not mandated by the Lau decision but was suggested as one alternative for redressing the rights of language minority children with limited English proficiency.

After Lau, the policy began to shift from language problems of the non-English-speaking children to the instructional problems faced by the schools in attempting to serve those children. Lau was important because it marked the beginning of a major policy shift that moves the responsibility for adapting to language differences from the home and the child to the school (González, 1994).

In 1975, the Office of Civil Rights published the Lau Remedies, guidelines that school districts should follow in order to comply with the Lau decision. The Lau Remedies were suggested guides to school districts in designing programs to overcome English language deficiencies, procedures for evaluating the English skills of second-language-learner children, and steps in establishing professional standards for bilingual and English as a Second Language (ESL) teachers. They specified that bilingual education had to be provided for non-English-speaking elementary school students who could not understand English. Only at the secondary level was ESL alone considered to be an appropriate program offering. Districts that refused to establish bilingual programs were no longer eligible for federal funding. As a consequence, school districts were encouraged to institute bilingual programs for two reasons: (a) Bilingual programs were the only programs that were eligible for government funding; and (b) bilingual programs were recommended by the Office of Civil Rights to provide equal educational opportunities to second-language-learner students required by law.

At the end of the Carter administration, the Lau Remedies were replaced by the Lau Regulations. These regulations had the force of law and required districts with 25 or more second-language-learner students of the same language group in two consecutive elementary grades to establish a bilingual program in that language. In 1981, Terrell Bell, Reagan's newly appointed secretary of education, withdrew the short-lived regulations as "harsh, inflexible, burdensome, unworkable, and incredibly costly rules." This action prevented the Lau Regulations from becoming a part of the Federal Register. Even though the Supreme Court's Lau decision did not require a specific instructional approach, the federal government does have a responsibility under that decision to ensure that school districts provide appropriate services for second-language-learner children (Crawford, 1997; Jiménez, 1992).

Although cases were litigated to ensure compliance with the Lau requirement for some special assistance, subsequent cases more often dealt with issues left unanswered in *Lau* v. *Nichols*.

In the decades of the 1970s and 1980s, litigation increased and has been an avenue of educational program reform that has produced significant changes in educational programs for second-language-learner students.

The Current Context of
Bilingual Education in the United States

A nation's political mood affects not only the nature of the educational policy debate but also the kind of research and instructional services that are funded and the research findings that receive the most attention. The current controversy over language is best understood in the context of a cyclical trend in the bilingualism debate.

During the early twentieth century, opposition to bilingualism derived strength from the then-dominant scientific wisdom. Studies in the field of education and psychology argued that bilingualism created failure, mental confusion, and damaged the psychological well-being of immigrant children and that the use of a foreign language at home created linguistic confusion of children exposed to two languages (Portes & Schauffler, 1996).

It was not until 1962 that these views were convincingly disproved by a methodologically sound study of the effects of bilingualism on cognitive ability. French- and English-speaking children in Canada were studied by Peal and Lambert (1962), who demonstrated that, if social class was taken into account, true bilingualism was associated with higher scores on a variety of intelligence tests (see also Cummins, 1981; Lambert and Tucker, 1972). True bilinguals, defined as those who could communicate competently in two languages, were shown to enjoy a greater degree of cognitive flexibility, superior concept formation, a diversified set of mental abilities, and an enhanced ability to deal with abstract concepts than their monolingual peers. Instead of creating confusion, having two symbols for each object enhanced understanding.

Despite accumulating factual evidence on the advantages of bilingualism, the opposition to bilingual education went further when Senator S. I. Hayakawa brought this issue into Congress in

1981. A critic of bilingual education and bilingual voting rights, Hayakawa introduced a constitutional amendment to make English the sole official language. The measure would have prohibited federal and state laws and policies from requiring the use of other languages (Hayakawa, 1992). His point was not only for English but also against bilingualism. By 1998, twenty-five states had made English their official language, either by amending their state constitutions or by enacting new legislation (U.S. English, 1999). By declaring English the official language all official documents, records, legislation and regulations, as well as hearings, ceremonies and public meetings are conducted solely in English (U.S. English, 1999).

Another indication of antibilingual sentiment is the large number of California residents who voted for Proposition 227, the "English for the Children" initiative. This proposition eliminates bilingual education and it was approved overwhelmingly at the polls (Banks, 2000).

A commonly used argument by those opposed to bilingual education is related to the design, implementation, and effectiveness of bilingual education programs. There is considerable inconsistency among the different types of programs in the use of the same term across different typologies and, at the same time, there is a proliferation of different terms for the same type of program. That is, researchers, politicians, journalists, and school administrators have used a wide variety of sometimes-conflicting terms to refer to program differentiation, with little sense of continuity or clarity.

Initially the most common bilingual program was the Transitional program, and more recently Maintenance and Enrichment programs have been advocated. In transitional classes, students of limited English proficiency receive instruction in their native language in all subject areas as well as instruction in English as Second Language, but only for a limited period of time. Native-language instruction is provided to avoid loss of grade-level skills while mastery of second language is taking place. As soon as students are considered proficient enough in English to work academically in all-English classes, they are moved from the bilingual program into monolingual classes with English-speaking students. Most transitional programs transfer students into all-English classes after a maximum of two to three years in bilingual classes

(Crawford, 1997; Lessow-Hurley, 2000). In such a short-term program there is less opportunity to mix English-speaking students with limited English-proficient students in academic tasks; thus, it is generally a segregated model. The highest priority of a transitional bilingual program is the teaching of English, with the goal of mainstreaming limited English-proficient students as soon as possible.

In the maintenance model, there is less emphasis on exiting students from the program as soon as possible. Students in maintenance bilingual classes receive content-area instruction in both languages equally throughout their school career, or for as many grades as the school system can provide the service. Maintenance programs at the secondary level are rare in the United States. Maintenance programs are based on an educational enrichment model; Transitional programs, on a compensatory model. The endpoint of maintenance education is to produce bilingual and biliterate students.

The maintenance model has prompted a controversy over how federal money should be spent. The main argument against bilingual education is that native-language maintenance is not the task of the federal government; that the development and maintenance of languages other than English are the responsibility of the parents and of voluntary cultural groups rather than of the public schools (Epstein, 1992; Glazer, 1989). However, maintenance bilingual education has become an issue of great political and economic significance for local communities that wish to maintain their ethnic heritage. This model creates a new source of income for bilingual teachers and aides hired by the school and thus is an economic incentive to upward mobility for the community.

Enrichment bilingual programs aim toward not only maintenance but also development and extension of the first language. Enrichment bilingual education is a term introduced by Fishman (1971) to refer to bilingual instruction for all members of society, rather than for minorities alone. Enrichment bilingual programs are based on the rationale that the processes of first and second language acquisition are similar. That is, acquisition occurs when students are exposed to natural language and they are motivated to communicate. Students in these programs are taught subject matter in two languages (teachers must be fully bilingual), rather than focusing on the language itself (as in foreign-language classes). This takes place over a period of years. The key is to provide comprehensible input, or understandable messages, through which children internalize grammar and vocabulary in the target language as they learn other academic subjects (Crawford, 1997). Enrichment programs assume a pluralistic model in that the goal is to make students bilingual and biliterate.

Recently there has been increasing attention in the United States to the dual or two-way bilingual program, which is a type of enrichment bilingual program. The dual bilingual program is an integrated model in which speakers of two languages are placed together in a bilingual classroom to learn each other's language and work academically in both languages. Most common in the United States are programs that simultaneously teach Spanish to English-background children and English to Hispanics, while cultivating the native-language skills of each group.

Charges of ineffectiveness have permeated bilingual education programs. The implementation of bilingual education programs has been affected by the uneven funding and interpretations provided by different political administrations. The federal role in the evaluation of the effectiveness of bilingual education for the Hispanic populations has been directed by political rather than by instructional concerns and, as result, has focused on a very narrow issue: whether or not bilingual education helps second-language-learner students to learn English faster.

Epstein (1992) argues that if students with English difficulties were to become well educated in English, as well as in their native language, most probably would find English the more useful language in this English-speaking society, and there would likely be a steady decrease in the use of the native language. Based on Epstein's argument undoubtedly, transitional programs would have the same effect, only sooner. There is a need for more reliable evidence that bilingual programs produce students who are well educated in English and in the native language.

Epstein continues his criticisms of bilingual education by pointing out that if the federal government is seeking to discover the best way to help students who do not speak English and who are doing poorly in school, a number of alternative courses are available. However, narrow definitions of eligible children are needed. That is, a generally accepted definition of the degree of English proficiency needed to learn in English is essential. It also would require written and oral language dominance tests to determine whether a student is better equipped to learn in the native language or in English.

The fact is that it is not the intention of bilingual educators to delay the acquisition of English. The value of acquiring English and acquiring it quickly is part of the bilingual discourse. Likewise is the battle against linking a lack of English proficiency with the ability to think logically, and therefore, secure democracy. Bilingual education done well gives positive results; bilingual education done badly gives poor results. Fluent bilingualism is an intellectual and cultural resource. In this sense, with a good bilingual program, there should not be incompatibility between learning English, preserving the native language, and fulfilling the American Dream.

The Hispanic Population in the United States

Today's new and rapidly accelerating immigration to the United States is extraordinary in its diversity of education level, culture, language and national origin. The 1990 population census counted 19.8 million immigrants, an all-time high. In terms of national origins, Latin American people constitute one of the largest immigrant populations in the country. Within this Spanish-speaking population there are differences in political perspective, phenotype, language dialect (though mutually intelligible), culture, migration histories, and modes of incorporation in the United States. Therefore, the one-size-fits-all label—such as Hispanic, Latino, and Chicano—deserves to be used with defined judgment.

In addition, it is important to distinguish among three distinct categories within the Spanish-speaking immigrant population in this country: immigrant children, children of immigrants, and native-born children of native-born parents. The first category includes children who are born abroad to parents born abroad and who come to the United States to be raised here. The second includes native-born children of immigrant parents. The third includes children born in the United States of native-born parents.

Regardless of the category, the term Hispanic includes any Spanish-speaking person, regardless of geographic or ethnic variation.

Research about these immigrants has focused largely on first-generation adults. However, even though much less is known about their children, they are a very visible presence in the schools and streets of many American communities and will form an increasingly important part of American society. Few studies have been conducted on the adaptation process of immigrant children and their prospects for the future, and what is known about their actual adaptation patterns is just in the early stages of inquiry. Much needed research can be traced to their self-identification, aspirations, cultural preferences, forms of intergenerational cohesion or conflict within their families, self-esteem, psychological well-being, and language shifts from the native language to English and bilingualism.

For children of immigrants, the developmental process of identity formation, educational attainment, and career prospects can be complicated by experiences of intense acculturation and intergenerational conflicts as they strive to adapt in a social-identity context that may be racially and culturally dissonant. According to the outcomes of a study developed by Rumbaut (1996), "becoming American" may take different forms, has different meanings, and is reached by different paths. But the process of defining an identity is one in which all children of immigrants are engaged. These children need to find a meaningful place in the society of which they are the newest members. The process is complex, conflictual, and stressful, and affects the consciousness of immigrant parents and children alike.

Growing up bicultural and bilingual is a difficult process, even under the best circumstances. Doing so in today's America is still a great challenge. According to data presented by Portes and Schauffler (1996) the typical language pattern has been for the first generation to learn enough English to survive economically; the second generation continued to speak the parental tongue at home but English in school, at work, and in public life; by the third generation, the home language shifted to English, which effectively became the mother tongue for subsequent generations.

This pattern has held true for most immigrants groups in the past with the exception of some isolated minorities. However, specifically in the case of the Hispanic group, the growing research about the positive effects of bilingualism as well the proliferation of the Hispanic self-contained communities may contribute to the emergence of other patterns of language preference and dominance. That is to say, possible patterns range from full language assimilation (English monolingualism), to fluent bilingualism, to full language retention (Spanish monolingualism).

Even though it is difficult to ascertain linguistic adaptation of immigrant children, some general notions in the sociology of immigration can be translated into the following expectations. Children growing up in sociocultural contexts where the native English-speaking majority is dominant or where immigrants from other linguistic backgrounds are most numerous will lose their home language faster and convert to English monolingualism more quickly. Conversely, those raised in contexts where a large bilingual concentration exists will have greater probability of parental language preservation. In such instances, there will be a clear economic incentive to retain proficiency in that language, along with greater facilities for learning and practicing it within the community. However, in some instances, the passage of time will lead eventually toward greater English proficiency and English preference and gradual abandonment of the native language (Portes & Schauffler, 1996). Inasmuch as policies promoting bilingualism as an intellectual and cultural resource are absent, this pattern will be perpetuated.

**Educational Attainment and
School Performance of Hispanic Students**
The literature concerning the educational attainment and performance of minority groups in the United States stresses that although most of minority students face special problems in school, some groups of minority students do comparatively well. For instance, according to the 1984 report of the U.S. Bureau of the Census, in the United States there is increasing evidence that students of Asian ancestry, both immigrant and U.S.-born, complete more years of education than their majority-group peers. Young people of Cuban ancestry also persist in school longer than non-Hispanic white Americans.

In addition, according to several research studies there is variability in school adjustment within different Hispanic groups. Hispanics of Central and South American origin, as well as those of Cuban origin, tend to do better in U.S. schools than their Mexican-American and mainland Puerto Rican peers. Newly arrived Puerto Ricans and Mexican immigrants tend to do better in school and have higher self-esteem than those who were born in the United States (Baral, 1979; Suárez-Orozco, 1987; Valverde, 1987).

From a socioanthropological perspective, voluntary immigrant minorities, such as Hispanics of Central and South American origin in the United States, generally perform better in schools and experience different kinds of problems than do involuntary, or castelike, minorities, such as African Americans, Mexican Americans, and Native Americans. Immigrant minorities are people who have moved more or less voluntarily to the United States because they believe that immigration will lead to greater economic well-being, better overall opportunities, or greater political freedom. Although the immigrants often experience difficulties due to language and cultural differences, they do not experience persistent school failure. Castelike or involuntary minorities, on the other hand, are people who were originally brought into United States society through slavery, conquest, or colonization. These minorities were relegated to servant positions and denied true assimilation into mainstream society (Ogbu, 1987, 1990). School performance and educational attainment is greatly influenced and affected by the minority group's perception of and responses to schooling, and that is related to its historical and structural experience in the larger society.

It is not unusual for students from castelike minorities to engage in what Ogbu (1986) calls "cultural inversion," that is, to resist acquiring and demonstrating the culture and the cognitive styles that are identified with the dominant group. Students from castelike minorities who engage in behaviors that correspond to the mainstream culture are frequently excluded by their peers. They must cope with the "burden of acting white." There is little benefit, in terms of peer relationships, in being successful students. Frequently, those who excel in school feel both internal ambivalence and external pressures not to manifest such behaviors and attitudes.

Not surprisingly, English-language competence and educational achievement have been significantly and positively correlated in the scholarship literature (Cummins, 1979, 1989; Rumbaut, 1996). The higher the English-language proficiency, the higher the academic achievement. In addition, knowledge of English can certainly have a very positive association with self-esteem and psychological well-being. Consequently, it can strongly be associated with higher educational aspirations, a fact that has never been in dispute in the arguments of bilingual education advocates. It is not the intention of bilingual instruction to delay the acquisition of English. Bilingual educators have never been skeptical regarding the value of acquiring English and acquiring it quickly. However, there should not be incompatibility between learning English and preserving the native language.

The effect of teachers' expectations on the academic achievement of minority groups has been documented as a strong influence on children's school performance. It seems to be that socioeconomic class has been related to the expectations the teachers hold for the children. In studies reported by Persell (1977) and Anyon (1981), expectations for poor children have been lower than for middle-class children, even when their IQs and achievement scores are similar. Teachers expect so little of low-class students that they are glad to get any work out of them at all. These beliefs became a rationale for providing low-level work in the form of elementary facts, simple drills, and memorization.

There is no mystery to tales of immigrant success or failure. School performance and educational attainment is explained as a multiplicity of competing and changing factors. The fates of immigrant children divide along lines of economic opportunity, social adjustment, educational aspirations, and bilingualism as an intellectual and cultural resource. The thrust of educational policy in the 1960s and 1970s was clearly one of providing access to those who were deprived of civil rights; the decades of the 1980s and 1990s ushered in a change of philosophy that switched concern from educational access to educational excellence. At the wake of the new millennium, the educational policy calls not only for a system embedded in the principles of excellence, but equity as well.

꧁꧂

Part II

Gifted Bilingual Education
in the United States

꧁

Chapter Two

Definitions and Conceptions of Giftedness in Bilingual Populations

"That our songs are different is nowhere near as important as the fact that we all have a song to sing"

F. Siccone (1995)

Some of the first questions that come to mind regarding gifted individuals are: What is giftedness? Is it inherited or acquired? Is it a rare characteristic in a chosen few or is it present in all human beings? Is it a narrow concept or does it encompass a multiplicity of abilities and skills? Although a definitive answer to these questions will not be finally determined in this text, I believe that there exists a hard-to-define quality (known as intelligence, potential, or talent) in gifted human beings that gives them the ability to acquire skills, become acclaimed performers, process information, and generate products within specific domains at a much higher level than those of the average population. I also believe that these abilities can be found in all ethnic, cultural, and linguistic groups and that socioeconomic stereotypes, ethnic prejudice, political climate, societal attitudes, and language can influence the identification and nurturance of this ability.

Understanding the causes for the acknowledged underrepresentation of children from culturally and linguistically different groups, particularly Hispanics, in programs for the gifted has been the focus of considerable research and reflection.

Reasons for their low representation vary, often reflecting a combination of factors related to the definition and conception of giftedness adopted and the identification procedure used. Depending on the criteria being used, there are some children who are slightly above-average while others are far above-average. Some seem to have talent potential in a single area while others appear to have potential in a variety of areas. Some individuals with talent potential seem to have little or no motivation to develop or use that capacity while others are highly interested, motivated, committed, and involved. Some children manifest an unusual talent potential at a very early age, while others show unusual performance much later in their development. Youngsters who are not identified and selected for inclusion in special programs are much less likely to be provided with the needed opportunities to nurture and develop their talent potential.

The gifted and talented are clearly a very multifaceted and heterogeneous group of individuals, and so are the different definitions and conceptions of giftedness. When dealing with a population of bilingual students, the definition and conception of giftedness is even more diverse and constitutes a complicated task, given that Hispanics in the United States do not constitute a homogeneous group. They represent a combination of people from different Spanish-speaking countries with distinctive characteristics. It is important to acknowledge the characteristics of the gifted bilingual population we are dealing with, since such characteristics will provide the foundation for a definition of giftedness, procedures for identification, and curriculum practices in a program for the gifted. Unfortunately very few and varied data exist on the characteristics of gifted bilingual students. Until more information is available, care must be taken in generalizing from those few data that exist.

One of the most influential studies regarding gifted Hispanic children, specifically Mexican American, was developed by Bernal (1974). Interestingly enough, the characteristics attributed to gifted Mexican American children were of a behavioral nature, instead of the cognitive view of intelligence as reflected by IQ scores and other single standardized measures. Such characteristics as rapid acquisition of the English language once exposed to it, leadership ability, constant interactions with older playmates, engagement in risk-taking behavior, ability to keep self-occupied and entertained, and being "street wise" were recognized by others as identifiers of a youngster who has the ability to "make it" in the American society.

Based on research done by Maker and Schiever (1989) the following list of characteristics can be found in gifted bilingual students: (a) communicates fluently with peers and within community, even if using nonstandard English; (b) requires touching, eye contact, feeling of support to achieve maximum academic productivity; (c) personal initiative, independent thought, and verbal aggressiveness, often inhibited in females; (d) nuclear and extended family closeness is highly valued; (e) able to function successfully in two cultures; and (f) accomplishes more, works better in small groups than individually.

In a survey conducted to assess the community's perceptions of characteristics of gifted Hispanic students, the following ten characteristics or indicators were associated with gifted Hispanic children: (a) finds many solutions to a problem; (b) likes to try new things; (c) is good at finding other uses for things; (d) is interested in a variety of things; (e) is observant; (f) is creative; (g) is curious; (h) likes to read; (i) is motivated to learn; and (j) asks questions (Bermúdez, Rakow, Márquez, Sawyer, and Ryan, 1991).

The three case studies included in this book complement and illustrate this discussion. All three students, their teachers, and their families referred to the students as verbal, curious, perceptive, alert, and social. They were also described as avid readers, as having superior drawing ability, as being able to rapidly acquire English language skills, as having superior communication ability, and as "different" from their classmates.

Not all gifted Hispanic students will exhibit the characteristics listed here. As previously stated, one cannot assume that all Hispanic students are alike. Each individual's characteristics, together with the cultural, social, economical, and political influences surrounding specific groups of Hispanics, vary. Educators must equip themselves with information regarding these variabilities or gifted bilingual children will hardly be referred as candidates for gifted programs.

The characteristics previously discussed give educators the opportunity to assess potential giftedness in bilingual populations

beyond the traditional single score framework. Traditional definitions of giftedness, like the one proposed by Terman (1926) as the
top one percent level in general intellectual ability as measured by
the Stanford-Binet Intelligence Scale or a comparable instrument,
perpetuated the notion of giftedness as synonymous with high IQ
for many years. Such narrow definitions of giftedness not only
have ignored the cultural, linguistic, and social characteristics of
Hispanic students but have restricted the number of them in
gifted programs as well.

The value of adopting a nontraditional definition of giftedness,
one that views giftedness more broadly, composed of a variety of
factors, more flexible, inclusive, and described within the context
of a particular culture, lies in the potential of identifying a greater
number of gifted children from bilingual populations. We as educators need to give every child the opportunity to sing his or her
song. We have to be there and ready to listen.

Chapter Three

Identification of Giftedness in Bilingual Children

There probably are as many different strategies and policies for identifying gifted and talented students as there are programs. Several assessment instruments are available which are well suited to gain reliable and comprehensive information about the gifted individual.

Among the most significant recommendations to create a defensible, pluralistic, comprehensive, and pragmatic identification system include the following: tailor the identification system according to the definition of giftedness adopted; use the identification system to select students whose potential is not sufficiently challenged by regular teaching and whose educational needs are not being met by the regular curriculum; design the identification system as a series of different steps including multiple criteria for identification (Borland, 1989; Borland & Wright, 1994; Renzulli, 1984; Tannenbaum, 1983). Recommendations like these should have had a significant and positive effect on addressing the underrepresentation of certain groups in programs for the gifted. Despite good intentions and good recommendations, however, problems in identifying gifted bilingual students continue to challenge educators.

The identification of gifted bilingual students is complex because it involves students who are both gifted and from a language and cultural background different from middle-class, native English-speaking children. In addition, these children come to school with different levels of English proficiency. Ascertaining the child's language dominance (preferred language) and language proficiency (actual linguistic ability) is a complicated process. There are some Hispanic children that are fully proficient in English; others are Spanish-monolingual; and others are in the process of developing a superficial mastery of English. In addition, one can make the mistake of assuming that all Hispanic children have Spanish language proficiency. Hispanic groups have different degrees of Spanish language exposure and usage.

When educators encounter the challenge of identifying gifted bilingual children, perceptions and judgments about the children's actual ability may be confounded by the children's cultural and language differences. Identification must be then based upon superior *potential* instead of superior performance.

Traditional identification practices frequently used in programs for gifted students can obscure their giftedness. Overreliance, misuse, and abuse of intelligence tests to make decisions about actual or potential giftedness has led to discriminatory tracking with bilingual children being identified less often as gifted than mainstream students.

The Use of Intelligence Tests
for Identifying Gifted Bilingual Children

For many years, children were identified as gifted either exclusively or primarily through intelligence tests. Even today, IQ scores serve as a major basis for identifying students for many gifted programs.

Intelligence tests have some features that not only give them a place in the current educational practice, but which also lead to their retention and continued use for identifying children with gifted potential. For instance, some argue that intelligence tests are good predictors of academic achievement (Borland, 1986; Kaufman & Harrison, 1986; Robinson & Chamrad, 1986; Thorndike & Hagen, 1986). If the main purpose of an identification process is to select those students with high academic ability or potential, certainly an IQ test can serve this purpose. As Sternberg (1986) pointed out "conventional IQ tests measure those analytic abilities needed in academic situations fairly well."

If we are to take into consideration characteristics such as attention span, language usage, anxiety, reaction to novel tasks, posture, and mood which can be observed during the administration of a test, then we can argue that intelligence tests yield more than just a score. In addition, intelligence tests yield a mental age estimate and provide normative information. The mental age estimate or rate of development may be useful in making a rough estimate of the child's chances of understanding material designed for older children as well as in comparing that student with others with similar characteristics. The mental age concept and the normative information can be useful in the classroom for program planning and designing purposes.

A proper role of IQ tests in programs for the gifted is to use them for purposes of inclusion, not exclusion (Borland, 1986; Richert, 1991). It is important to use the information provided by IQ tests when it reflects well on children. A low IQ score may be a poor or misleading indicator of student ability if the child comes from a culturally and linguistically different environment. One of the case studies presented in this book (Tina) proves to be a witness for such a practice. In Tina's case, a low score on a standardized intelligence test did not rule out the possibility of giftedness.

Despite the positive aspects of IQ tests, in recent years there has been a different perception among educators that an IQ is not enough to measure intelligence and that an individual's intellectual ability cannot be represented by a single score. Intelligence is something richer, more complex, and more extensive than the mental process required to achieve a high IQ score.

When using standardized tests with any group of students, low motivation, poor reading skills, differing cognitive styles, or poor test taking skills may mask high achievement. Additionally, with second-language-learner students, several problems may arise with the child's background knowledge and past experiences as well as with English competency needed (Cárdenas, 1995; Cummins, 1984; Ford & Harris, 1990; González, 1974; Melesky, 1985; Woods & Achey, 1990). When the individual's language and life experiences are different from those represented in the test, undoubtedly a low test score will result and the individual's true ability and potential will be underestimated.

In order to overcome this problem, test makers have attempted to produce tests that do not depend upon language or upon a specific cultural background. In fact several authors recommend the use of such measures to improve identification decisions (Bernal, 1978; Eby & Smutny, 1990; Ford & Harris, 1990; Frasier, 1993; Melesky, 1985; Ortiz & Volloff, 1987; Richert, 1991; Zappia, 1989). Such tests include: the Cartoon Conservation Scales (DeAvila, Struthers, & Randall, 1969); the Goodenough-Harris Drawing Test (Harris, 1963); the Raven's Coloured Progressive Matrices (Raven, 1965); the SOI-Learning Abilities Test (Meeker & Meeker, 1986); and the Torrance Test of Creative Thinking (Torrance, 1974).

However, some authors (Arvey, 1972; Kitano & Kirby, 1986; Sattler, 1992) argue that people from different cultural backgrounds do not always perform any better on culture-fair tests than on the more conventional tests, and that attempts to create culture-fair tests have not been successful (Borland & Wright, 1994; Kitano & Kirby, 1986). According to Sattler (1992) probably no test can be created that will entirely eliminate the influence of learning and cultural experiences. The test content, the materials, the language in which the questions are phrased, the test directions, the scoring criteria, and the validity criteria are all culture-bound.

In further attempt to make intelligence tests more appropriate for second-language-learner children, specifically Hispanic children, test makers translated and modified some intelligence tests. For example, there are Spanish versions of the Kaufman Assessment Battery for Children (Kaufman & Kaufman, 1983); the System of Multicultural Pluralistic Assessment (SOMPA) (Mercer & Lewis, 1978); the Wechsler Intelligence Scale for Children-Revised (Wechsler, 1974); and the Woodcock-Johnson Psychoeducational Battery (Woodcock, Johnson, Mather, McGrew, & Werder, 1977).

The fact of having such translated versions, however, does not signify that the problem of using IQ tests with bilingual children is solved. In fact, test translations have some inherent difficulties. For instance such adapted versions are sometimes just translations of tests used in other countries that were not written with the bilingual child in mind from a linguistic nor a cultural point of view.

In addition, given that the Hispanic population in the United States encompasses people from many different Spanish-speaking countries, with several Spanish dialects (though mutually intelligible), the Spanish translation of an intelligence test would have to be linguistically appropriate (Bernal, 1981b; Cárdenas, 1995). That is, it would have to include the dialect that the child speaks. The word "kite," for example, may be translated as *cometa, huila, volantin, papalote, or chiringa,* depending on the country of origin. If the dialect or regional variations are not taken into account, the attempt to validate intelligence tests through translations would be futile.

Many concepts in standardized tests either have no equivalent in another language or are difficult to translate without causing ambiguity. Thus, the meaning of important phrases may be lost in translations.

Some words may have different meanings for Puerto Ricans, Cubans, Mexicans, and other Hispanics. For example, *tostón* means a half dollar to a Mexican child but a squashed section of a fried banana to a Dominican child.

The level of difficulty of words may change as a result of a literal translation (Cárdenas, 1995; Sattler, 1992). For instance, the Spanish equivalent of the common English word "pet" is *animal doméstico,* which is not only a difficult word but very uncommon as well.

Studies designed to investigate the effect of Spanish translations of intelligence tests and vocabulary tests reveal inconsistent data. The Spanish test version may result in higher, similar, or even lower scores than the English version (Bergan & Parra, 1979; Cárdenas, 1995; Chavez, 1982; Myers & Goldstein, 1979; Palmer & Graffney, 1972; Sattler & Altes, 1984). So test translations do not guarantee more valid results.

Further problems may arise when analyzing and interpreting test scores of translated versions and culture-fair tests. The quality and quantity of normative (comparative) data accompanying standardized tests is the key to interpreting test scores. Norms allow the comparison and interpretation of an individual's score relative to groups of comparable students, so if Spanish versions and culture-fair tests use the original United States norms for determining scaled scores and IQ equivalents for bilingual examinees, the interpretation of the data will be inaccurate.

The argument that national norms are inappropriate for ethnic minority children has led some writers, like Mercer (1976), for example, to advocate establishing pluralistic norms. Those who favor pluralistic norms believe that it is useful to know how a child's performance compares to that of others in his or her own ethnic group. However, pluralistic norms are potentially dangerous because they provide a basis for inappropriate comparisons among different ethnic groups. Furthermore, Bernal (1980) argues that the renorming of tests to devise pluralistic norms is inappropriate because it does not involve test modifications. The use of pluralistic norms gives rise to new questions, like what norms should be used for a child who was born in the United States, has a Mexican father, and has a French mother?

Despite criticisms and limitations of intelligence tests, several schools are still relying on them as a major tool in the identification of children for gifted programs. If that is the case, then standardized tests must be used correctly, with an awareness of their limitations and must be selected carefully and used wisely. The user needs to know how children from specific ethnic groups perform on the test that has been selected. A high score on an intelligence test deserves further consideration, but a low score should not rule out the possibility of giftedness. Test results should be interpreted in light of the child's cultural background and primary language and should be interpreted in relation to other data, never in isolation.

Other Recommended Practices
for Identifying Gifted Bilingual Children

Many researchers and practitioners recommend the use of multiple assessment measures to give bilingual students several opportunities to demonstrate their skills and performance potential. These assessment measures include the following:

Teacher, Parent, Peer, and Self-recommendations

The different types of recommendations represent judgments based on observations of the child's behavior in more naturalistic conditions. This process allows for a broad range of giftedness if the nominators have been trained with specific information on the identification of special populations of gifted students. Otherwise, nominations may be limited in pointing out talents beyond the stereotypical traits associated with giftedness.

Teacher recommendations. Teachers have the opportunity to make observations of the student in the classroom and to judge how he or she accomplishes different kinds of tasks or how he or she reacts to different learning situations. Teachers are therefore able to make judgments about how a particular child's abilities compare to those of other children of the same age. However, when classroom achievement does not reflect the abilities expected, teacher recommendations may not accurately reflect potentially gifted students.

In their study, Pegnato and Birch (1959) found that junior high school teachers not only failed to nominate over 50 percent of the gifted individuals in the school, but they also identified many average students as gifted. Teachers may select the hardworking student instead of the active, noncompliant students who might really be the most gifted. Additionally, according to the data presented by Schack and Starko (1990), "teacher pleasers" are more likely to be nominated for gifted programs, while other gifted students may never be considered because they do not display these "lesson-learning" characteristics in the classroom.

Several rating scales have been developed to help teachers become more effective identifiers of gifted students. Teachers are asked to indicate the presence or absence and the frequency of certain behaviors thought to be indicative of giftedness. Probably the most widely used teacher rating scale is Renzulli and Hartman's (1971) Scale for Rating Behavioral Characteristics of Superior Students (SRBCSS). The scale asks teachers to rate students on 8 to 10 items in each of four areas: learning, motivation, creativity, and leadership. Ratings are made in terms of the frequency of observed behaviors on a scale 1 to 4. The 1976 version of the SRBCSS (Renzulli, Smith, White, Callahan, & Hartman, 1976) includes six additional scales: artistic, musical, dramatics, communication precision, communication expressiveness, and planning.

Although the SRBCSS is available commercially, care must be exercised when using it. According to Borland (1989), it is very unlikely that this or any other scale will fit the needs of every identification program. He suggests that school personnel should examine this and other rating scales and develop their own instruments that will better fit the needs of their program. Borland and Wright (1994), for instance, use a teacher nomination form as part of their screening process for identifying potentially gifted, economically disadvantaged young children, which only asks the teachers to nominate the children they feel should be looked at more closely and to indicate why the children are being nominated.

With second-language-learner students, teacher recommendations have also shown to be unreliable and sometimes ineffective. The failure of teachers to identify gifted bilingual students accurately may be caused by several factors. One of such factors is the teachers' inability to recognize behavior indicative of giftedness in bilingual students. Tuttle and Becker (1980) pointed out that teachers usually tend to emphasize such behaviors as neatness, punctuality, answering correctly, and cooperation which are not necessarily traits of gifted individuals. According to Schack and Starko (1990), teachers' reliance on classroom performance aspects also may contribute to the underrepresentation of culturally different students in gifted programs. Nomination opportunities could be missed if the talent of bilingual students lies in areas other than those contributing to traditional school success.

Finally, a third factor contributing to the failure of teachers to accurately identify giftedness in bilingual students is the teacher's attitude and/or expectations toward bilingual individuals, which, unfortunately, in some cases tends to be negative. Without adequate knowledge of the impact of culture on behavior, teachers often do not understand the motivation behind the actions of bilingual students and, therefore, overlook children for gifted programs. Also, teachers may assume a student is not gifted based on his or her language proficiency, use of nonstandard English, accent, differing values, aspirations, and levels of motivation.

Fortunately, teachers may be trained to more accurately identify gifted bilingual students. In-service training sessions on the characteristics and behaviors of these children, as well as student profiles or case study examples of gifted bilingual students, may be utilized to increase teacher awareness of talents and gifts among bilingual students.

Parent recommendations. Parents are in the best possible position to act as observers and recorders of their children's behavior. Parents can provide information about the child's interests, hobbies, and developmental history. They also have the opportunity to observe their children in more relaxed, informal situations, and in a much wider variety of settings than do teachers (e.g., at play, in after-school and weekend activities, at school events). However, parents, and especially Hispanics, may not always play an active role in the referral process for gifted programs. In a study conducted by Scott, Perou, Urbano, Hogan, and Gold (1992), it was reported that fewer minority parents than white parents refer their children for possible inclusion in gifted programs. These data suggest that the underrepresentation of Hispanic children in programs for the gifted may, in part, relate to the differential role their parents currently play in the referral process.

According to Woods and Achey (1990), most parents may not have the necessary background and knowledge about assessment procedures and special programs in the schools to become an advocate for their children. Also, parent-school interaction is sometimes hampered by the parent's modesty, language differences, mistrust, and defensive attitudes.

Another important aspect that needs to be considered when using parent recommendations is that most parents may not always be able to interpret or evaluate what they observe. A fact that cannot be overlooked when dealing with Hispanic parents is that since gifted education is not fully developed throughout the Spanish-speaking countries as it is in the United States, it is possible that some of the parents have not heard of or have not had contact with gifted education in their home countries and are, therefore, unaware of the characteristics of a gifted child as well as the advantages and benefits of a program for gifted children. Consequently, their recommendations for placement in a gifted program may not be accurate and reliable.

Parent recommendations are critical because many gifted bilingual students may not be performing in school at an academic level that would alert the teachers to their superior abilities, or their differing cognitive styles, language differences, low motivation, or poor test taking skills may mask high achievement. The use of parent recommendations can be enhanced through a public education program which alerts parents to those characteristics which might indicate giftedness and which informs them about the availability and function of educational programs for gifted students.

Peer recommendations. Peers are another valuable source of information and they can provide important insights into the abilities of other children. Usually, teachers' perception of student ability is limited to contact within the classroom and as an adult to a child. Student contact with classmates may allow for more demonstration of characteristics such as leadership ability, creative approaches to maintenance, and survival (i.e., coping in the home environment and neighborhood).

A very popular technique for gathering information about leadership is the sociogram, a technique that traditionally has been used to assess social relations among persons in a classroom or group situation. Renzulli, Reis, and Smith (1981) reported that a variation on the sociogram technique has been used effectively to nominate students for participation in programs for the gifted.

Self-recommendations. The individual himself or herself is a valuable source of information. Numerous authors suggest the use of self-nominations, especially for some types of information such as personal aspirations, interests, motivation, feelings, beliefs, and preferences (Borland, 1989; Hagen, 1980; Richert, 1991; Robisheaux & Banbury, 1994; Tannenbaum, 1983; Zappia, 1989).

The information can be obtained in the form of a checklist of characteristics; biographical inventories; yes/no questions, which are especially helpful with younger children; or interviews.

Student Records

The student's cumulative file can be a good source for obtaining the educational history of an individual. Such files contain information on academic achievement, general scholastic aptitudes, interests, teachers' comments, grade point averages, and in the case of a second-language-learner students, his or her language preference.

Even though the use of existing records constitute a good option for obtaining information about gifted bilingual students, care must be taken when analyzing the information. Grades can be as misleading as they are helpful. Grades often reflect perceptions of appropriate classroom behavior rather than actual ability. Furthermore, good grades may sometimes be associated with high achievement as well as with conformity and teacher pleasing. On the contrary, low grades do not necessarily impede a lack of or limited ability, but may indicate a lack of motivation or heavy emphasis by the grader on non-achievement factors such as attitude or class attendance. Finally, some bright students may desire to "fit in" by earning low or average marks since grades may reflect the level of educational aspiration in the home, peer pressure, or lack of successful educational role models.

Gifted program directors need to be sensitive to cultural and language factors affecting bilingual students' performance in order to escape misleading assumptions that accompany low grades.

Student Portfolios

Within the field of education, portfolio assessment has been used as an alternative approach to assess writing. In fact, the word *portfolio*, traditionally speaking, refers to a collection of a student's writing samples over a number of occasions (Camp & Levine, 1991; Glazer, Brown, Fantauzzo, Nugent, & Searfoss, 1993; Knight & Gallaro, 1994). This definition and the whole philosophy of this mode of alternative assessment has been broadened and applied in many academic areas and disciplines, such as art, theater, photography, early childhood education (see Knight & Gallaro, 1994), and gifted education (see Wright & Borland, 1993).

The use of portfolios holds particular promise in the identification of giftedness in special populations, especially when an overdependence on traditional measures utilized in screening for gifted programs has provided a limited portrait of the student ability and potential.

Within the context of gifted education, a portfolio is defined as a systematic and purposeful collection of student work and records, that "document the child's status and growth in one or more developmental domains" (Wright & Borland, 1993). Portfolios invite us to look at what students can do, not what they cannot; they can provide an accurate measure of what students have accomplished. Also, portfolios can reinforce students' own learning process and help them set goals for future learning.

This student work sample can include virtually any product prepared by a student, written, oral, or behavioral. However, a portfolio should be an integral reflection of the program goal rather than a random sampling of products and activities. Following are possible examples of products to be included in portfolios:

Writings. Through an examination of student writings, it is possible to gain an awareness of students' knowledge, vocabulary, emergent literacy, analytical reasoning, creativity, sensitivity to issues, and fine motor development. Writing samples can be collected from different settings and can be of various types such as compositions, letters, reports, stories, or other materials written by hand, dictated to a peer or adult, orally recorded and transcribed, or composed on a computer.

Artwork. These types of products are very valuable when trying to make judgments on originality and creativity, as well as on student developmental level and interests. When assessing children's artwork, it is important to consider if common or unusual materials are used in new or different ways; the presence of persistent themes; and experimentation with style, form, shape, and color. Renzulli (1977) recommends that students' products, especially artwork, be displayed before a real and appropriate audience. The audience may consist of peers, parents, artists, and other members of the school community.

Art samples aid in the identification process of bilingual children for gifted programs, by allowing them to demonstrate their talents and gifts in a meaningful way. Moreover, art provides a powerful nonverbal way of communication.

Photographs, videotapes and audiotapes. Photos and recordings of students' projects and performances supply data to further investigate a child's ability, especially when no paper product or tangible outcome is involved. Also, periodic photographs of a student's work may be used to document complex and sophisticated ideas.

The content as well as the implementation of student portfolios varies. There are no fixed steps for their implementation nor there are predetermined type of products that needed to be included in the portfolio; the process is highly individualized.

With regard to its implementation, several authors agree on the fact that it is a process that demands time and energy (Hadaway & Marek-Schroer, 1992; Kingore, 1995; Wright & Borland, 1993). Teachers and staff must be committed and interested in implementing such a process and be aware that problems and difficulties will be encountered even when implementation is ultimately successful.

Some suggestions for its implementation and management include: provide sufficient time for in-service education and preparation prior to its implementation, and also provide support during the actual implementation; schedule a series of parent-teacher conferences to discuss and reflect upon what is contained in the portfolio, to give parents concrete evidence of their children's progress in a specific area, and also to encourage parental involvement and support of their child's abilities; schedule a series of child-teacher conferences to give children a sense of their own learning and growth; schedule child-child conferences in order to allow children to take pride in their work and to have it taken seriously by their peers; keep the portfolio simple, keep the folders accessible to children, data all entries, and use summary sheets on the portfolio for teacher, peer, and student comments on outcomes; and finally, add to each product a student's statement and justification for the reason the piece was included (Glazer, Brown, Fantauzzo, Nugent, & Searfoss, 1993; Kingore, 1995; Wright & Borland, 1993).

The content of a student portfolio varies from setting to setting. Some teachers will have extremely structured ideas for what is to be included. Others may have students include all their work turning the portfolio into a pile, rather than a file of selected work and making the volume of material overwhelming. Teachers need to decide which samples best represent accomplishments, and which provide the best information for further planning instruction. In other words, teacher-selected samples should communicate the student's ability, potential, or growth in a selected domain.

In some settings student input concerning product selection might be allowed. Student involvement is a great source of information on decision-making capability. In addition, this encourages students to think critically about their work; it communicates to them that their work is taken seriously; and it encourages reflective attitudes.

The best approach regarding product selection is a blend of teacher and student input. This will yield the most comprehensive portrait of a child's development, process and product.

When evaluating the student portfolio, as with any other identification measure, an area of concern is teacher bias and unfamiliarity with a student's cultural and language background. Teachers and school staff need to be aware of the characteristics of gifted bilingual children and, perhaps, for evaluation purposes, several evaluators or experts might be required. This might be a long and time-consuming process; however, it is very important to evaluate appropriately the multiple modes of expression that the student portfolio allows.

Teacher Observations

Interest in assessment methods that are more open-ended and more naturalistic is growing. With the use of systematic observations (observation using a particular system) a vast amount of information can be obtained about the child's ability; creativity; play behavior; social, emotional, physical, cognitive, and language development.

Observations can be obtained informally through the use of checklists or rating scales, where the presence or absence of certain traits or behaviors is indicated, or through anecdotal records; running records; or formal time samples of frequency, rate, and duration of behaviors (see Beaty, 1998; Boehm & Weinberg, 1997).

It is important that the child be observed during a number of occasions and in as many situations as possible to obtain a more representative sample of the child's behavior; to understand patterns of behavior; to determine student performance; to detect behavior that suggests potential giftedness; to determine student's use of language (range of vocabulary, precision in the use of words, and complexity of sentence structure); and in the case of bilingual students, to observe language preference and proficiency in both languages.

Although observations constitute an appropriate and valuable source of information when identifying gifted bilingual students, there are still some concerns related to its validity, reliability and subjectivity (Borland, 1994; Hagen, 1980; Richert, 1991; Thorndike & Hagen, 1986). Unfortunately, gathering valid, reliable, and objective observational data is not an automatic, common-sense activity. There are many factors that can distort the value of the information gathered—for example, observer bias; observer expectations of student's ability; inadequate training on the observational system being used; and observer's lack of information about the behavioral characteristics of giftedness in bilingual students (Bermúdez & Rakow, 1990; Bernal, 1981a; Boehm & Weinberg, 1997; Woods & Achey, 1990).

It is possible to increase objectivity, validity, and reliability of observational data by developing systematic training and practice sessions on the observational system used; by providing training sessions on the characteristics and behaviors indicative of giftedness in bilingual populations; and by sampling behavior over time and under several situations to eliminate the tendency to draw conclusions from insufficient evidence.

The multiple assessment approach provides a vast amount of data regarding the child. It is important, however, to recognize that it is not always the case that more is better. The multiple assessment approach does not necessarily guarantee making valid decisions. According to Feldhusen and Jarwan (1993), the question to be asked, therefore, is not how many measures are used in the identification process, but rather what contribution each piece of information has to making valid decisions or to serving specific objectives. It is a waste of money, time, and effort to collect data that is not going to be used or that is not contributing to a better understanding and evaluation of the child. The goal is to have a variety of measures that complement each other in order to find diverse indicators of potential that a single measure cannot reflect.

The addition of other criteria to address the multiple dimensions of giftedness, as well as to accommodate children for whom the detection of their gifted abilities does not fit the traditional formula for identification, is a valuable asset. However, these assessment criteria should and must be viewed as valuable alternatives, not just additives to the traditional identification procedure.

Once the information has been gathered, a case study approach might be appropriate for the placement decision. Placement involves a decision for a special program that will better meet the academic needs of a certain child. This decision is very important since it affects the child, his or her family, the school, and the society as well. Consequently, the case study approach is appropriate because it involves a careful review of all available information by an appropriate group of educators who are knowledgeable of and affected by the program for the gifted. The composition of such a committee is determined by the type of program; for example, music and art educators have to be part of the committee if the special program stresses artistic creativity.

The decision committee that will select bilingual children for special programs needs to include educators who know and understand the gifted bilingual child. It is important to keep in mind that bias is not limited to the identification measures themselves. Bias permeates the entire decision-making process, interpretation of identification results, determination of eligibility, and recommendation for placement. Educators must be aware of the fact that bilingual students might express their talent in a way other than those usually expected by school personnel.

Project Synergy: A Non-traditional Identification Process

Various research projects awarded under the Jacob Javits Gifted and Talented Students Program have developed a number of initiatives that attempt to provide a foundation of research and practice on the underidentification and underrepresentation of economically disadvantaged children from ethnic minority groups in programs for gifted students. Project Synergy represents one such initiative. The portraits included in this book are the result of such an identification process.

Project Synergy (see Borland, 1994; Borland & Wright, 1994) operated from 1991 through 1996. The identification process included a screening phase, a diagnostic assessment phase, and a case study and placement decision phase. Multiple sources of information were used, including the following: observations, group enrichment activities, draw-a-person activity, teacher nominations, information from the parents, standardized tests, literature-based activities, and a child interview. Once the children were identified, intervention began, which included transitional services (Borland, 1994), mentorships with gifted adolescents (Wright & Borland, 1992), and parent seminars (Davis-Simons, 1995).

In September 1993, a new project began operation as an outgrowth of Project Synergy: Project Synergy Preschool. This new project extended Project Synergy's goals to a preschool population. Project Synergy Preschool operated from 1993 through 1995. Intervention was also provided for these children. Both for Project Synergy and Project Synergy Preschool, placement in classes for gifted students was the long-term goal.

Several children were identified as potentially gifted using the process of Project Synergy, including the children highlighted in Part III (see Kogan-Frenk, 1997). Project Synergy's and Project Synergy Preschool's identification process adhered to important and solid principles. It was equitable in that no student was overlooked; strategies were specified for identifying gifted children from different cultural and linguistic backgrounds; it was done in the early years of the students' academic careers thus permitting an earlier intervention and support; it was pluralistic since a broad definition and conception of giftedness was used; it was pragmatic because the identification procedures allowed for modifications to accommodate the needs of the children being identified. The impact of this identification process can be seen in the portraits included in this book. It was strong and long-lasting. All three families learned and grew together with their children.

❧

Chapter Four

The Education of
Gifted Bilingual Students

During the past two decades, the debate about program development for gifted children has been in response to the general question: what type of curriculum is appropriate for gifted students? Certainly an organized curriculum is a key ingredient in the transformation of a gifted individual's high performance into a mature competence for academic and professional accomplishment. Although this quest generated multiple responses, reflecting the wide variety of definitions and conceptions of the term gifted, it showed little disagreement over the need for a differentiated curriculum for gifted children. According to Passow (1982) there are seven guiding principles of curriculum differentiation for gifted and talented students. Curricula for gifted and talented students should:

1. Focus on and be organized to include more elaborate, complex, and in-depth study of major ideas, problems, and themes that integrate knowledge with and across systems of thought.
2. Allow for the development and application of productive thinking skills to enable students to reconceptualize existing knowledge and/or generate new knowledge.
3. Enable students to explore constantly changing knowledge and information and develop the attitude that knowledge is worth pursuing in an open world.

4. Encourage exposure to, selection, and use of appropriate and specialized resources.
5. Promote self-initiated and self-directed learning and growth.
6. Provide for the development of self-understandings and the understanding of one's relationship to persons, societal institutions, nature, and culture.
7. Should be evaluated in accordance with prior stated principles, stressing higher-level thinking skills, creativity, and excellence in performance and products.

Passow's principles seem very comprehensive, encompassing most of the curriculum modifications and adaptations suggested by other educators concerned with curriculum planning for gifted students (see Borland, 1989; Clark, 1997; Eliason & Jenkins, 1994; Gallagher, 1994; Maker, 1982; Tannenbaum, 1983; VanTassel-Baska, 1989).

Borland (1989) suggests some formal requirements for developing a curriculum that should not only be differentiated, but defensible as well. First, there should be consensus about what gifted students should learn that they would not learn in mainstream. Second, there should be a scope and sequence, an epistemological structure, to provide a meaningful organization for the knowledge as well as to serve as a basis for planning instruction. Last, there should be articulation with the core curriculum.

Borland points out that even the presence of these requirements is not enough to guarantee a defensible curriculum. In addition, emphasis on the development of thinking processes, appropriate and meaningful content, opportunities for independent study, provisions for acceleration, and curricula developed by the teachers who will implement them are, according to him, some of the other features necessary to make a curriculum for gifted students both differentiated and defensible.

Another aspect of curriculum planning for gifted children that has received vast attention is grouping arrangements. A wide variety of scheduling and grouping modifications exists in special instruction for gifted students: from modest changes in the program within the regular classroom, to part-time experiences during the school day, to separation from the regular program in special classes or special schools. In other words, students identified as gifted may receive some form of curricular differentiation by the regular classroom teacher, or they may be pulled out from their regular classroom for a given period of time each day for special instruction with other gifted students, or they may even be grouped with other gifted students for special classes in those subject areas in which they demonstrate high achievement. If a more homogeneous grouping option is desired, then the gifted students can be placed in self-contained classes for gifted students only or in a separate self-contained school designed exclusively for children identified as gifted.

Struggling with the issue of providing differentiated learning experiences for students with gifts and talents, educators have also proposed a wide variety of teaching-learning models for designing programs for the gifted. For example, there are models designed as a total enrichment program for the gifted like Renzulli's Enrichment Triad Model (Renzulli & Reis, 1986); models that focused on the development of cognitive and affective processes such as Bloom's Taxonomy (Bloom & Krathwohl, 1982) and Kohlberg's Moral Development Model (Kohlberg, 1982); models that have the affective domain as a major focus like Williams' Cognitive-Affective Interaction Model (Williams, 1982) or Bett's Autonomous Learner Model (Betts, 1986); models that provide a variety of thinking processes like Guilford's Structure of Intellect Model (Guilford, 1982); and systematic procedures for organizing and delivery of instructional strategies such as Taba's Teaching Strategies Program (Taba, 1982).

There is no one right way to teach gifted children. No single approach to meeting the needs of the gifted can possibly be right for all schools and all communities. The decision as to which scheduled or grouped strategies, or teaching-learning models, are most appropriate should be determined by the student's characteristics and special educational needs as well as upon the availability of specially trained staff, the number of gifted students identified, the physical facilities, provisions for transporting the children, and the general educational philosophy as represented in the school district. Programs and practices for the gifted need to be carefully planned, designed, implemented, and evaluated in order to maximize their potential effect.

Educational Service Delivery
for Gifted Bilingual Students

Standards of a qualitatively different, appropriate, and defensible curriculum for the gifted, as well as grouped strategies and models for designing the program, apply to all gifted students, regardless of social, economic, or cultural background. In other words, educational services offered to gifted bilingual students should meet already established standards and educational goals designed for all gifted students. However, when dealing with gifted bilingual children, a special program cannot be claimed to be defensible and appropriate solely by adhering to such criteria. Gifted bilingual education must take into account other important criteria as well: the language, cultural values, needs, and interests of the gifted children who are going to be served by the program. As Bernal (1976) stresses, "a gifted program suitable for bilingual children should utilize the cultural values represented and the various language or dialectical varieties found among its student members". It is very important, Bernal adds, that the diverse learning styles found in different individuals or cultural groups should also be incorporated into the curriculum design.

A key concept to serve gifted bilingual students successfully is individualization. Individualization is not exclusive for gifted bilingual students. In fact, individualization is a concept deeply ingrained in the philosophy of gifted education. Passow (1980) urged that educators should provide experiences which are appropriate and adequate in terms of each student's unique nature and needs. Maker (1983) adds that the process of individualization involves the development of a curriculum based on an assessment of the student's strengths and weaknesses. So an individualized program should be a reflection of the modifications necessitated by the unique learning needs evidenced by the gifted bilingual student.

Suggestions for Teachers

The literature on the educational needs of gifted bilingual children stresses the following recommendations as an integral part of the curriculum:

Use familiar concrete materials as teaching tools and hands-on learning experiences to teach abstract concepts. Bilingual students, particularly from impoverished homes, lack much of the stimulation and exposure needed to develop abstract academic concepts and, as a result, need concrete materials to manipulate when learning abstract concepts (Udall, 1989). Gradually the teacher can move from concrete to abstract materials and examples. For instance, when teaching the concept of classification, the teacher might begin by using known and tangible objects (e.g., puzzles, geoboards, tangrams, balance scales) and later introduce words, concepts, and ideas. However, it is very important, according to Udall (1989), that the teacher clearly understands the higher level concept being taught and how the manipulative used can develop a child's understanding of the concept. Otherwise, students do little more than play with materials and do not generalize to the underlying concept.

According to the analysis of the research findings on successful interventions with disadvantaged gifted learners across several study areas done by VanTassel-Baska, Patton, and Prillaman (1989), using familiar concrete objects as teaching tools and hands-on learning techniques appear to work well with disadvantaged gifted students.

Incorporate basic skills training if necessary. Frequently, nonacculturated Hispanic students, particularly those who are monolingual Spanish speakers with language-related difficulties, will enter programs for the gifted with fewer basic skills than their Anglo-American peers (M. Farr, program coordinator of "Providing Enrichment for Able Kids," personal communication, September 22, 1995; Udall, 1989). Developing a transition or trial placement program that highlights basic skills training in reading and language might be one option (Maker, 1983; Melesky, 1985). Incorporating communication and language skills training into the existing program for the gifted might be another.

Use creative and problem-solving strengths. Some writers have noted that creativity and problem solving are strengths that can be developed effectively in the classroom when dealing with gifted Hispanic children (Bernal, 1976; Feldhusen & Treffinger, 1985; Maker, 1983; Schulkind, 1982; Torrance, 1977; Udall, 1989). Torrance (1977) identified creative characteristics that frequently appear among disadvantaged children and upon which programs for the gifted might successfully be created. These include high nonverbal fluency and originality; high creative productivity in small groups; adeptness in visual art activities; high creativity in movement, dance, and other physical activities; high motivation for games, music, sports, humor, and concrete objects; and rich imagery in language. Torrance states, as confirmed by Bermúdez et al. (1991), that among the strengths of gifted disadvantaged students are brainstorming, creative problem solving, and small group work.

One should use the creative strengths of Hispanic students to encourage cognitive growth and intellectual pursuits by integrating creativity development with the teaching of curriculum content.

Use examples that are relevant to culture and experience. According to Taba and Elkins (1968), the cultural and social factors that affect learning must be understood in order to create curricular experiences that are meaningful, relevant, and worthwhile for the students for whom they are intended. They argue that relevancy is the cornerstone of motivation. Using concrete examples from students' experiences, from topics about which they are knowledgeable and from areas of intrinsic interest, will make the curriculum relevant.

There are a number of opportunities for some changes in existing curricula that could make the material more relevant and interesting to the culturally diverse student. One is a well-stocked library and classroom reference shelves that contain literature, history, and anthropology relevant to the cultural groups in that area.

Concentrate on affective needs. The affective needs of gifted Hispanic students, in particular the development of a positive self-esteem, should have a special emphasis in the curriculum. According to Udall (1989), a high and positive self-esteem will occur when students learn to handle the conflicts caused by the demands of two cultures, and also when they establish a strong self-identity while maintaining a cultural identity. Having a multicultural component in the curriculum can lead to a greater understanding of both differences and similarities in cultures and, in turn, will encourage a strong sense of pride and identity.

Include leadership training as an important part of the curriculum. Authors like Lamb and Busse (1983), Udall (1989), and Willings (1983) believe that many students have leadership talent that is never tapped. Lamb and Busse (1983) pointed out that it is unfortunate that in the regular classroom little conscious direct leadership training occurs. Leadership skills can be taught and instruction should begin in the early years. Several studies describe leadership development activities with young children based on social sensitivity, problem solving, conflict resolution, role taking, and creative drama (Edwards, Logue & Russell, 1983; Fuchigami, 1978; Hensel, 1991; Willings, 1983).

Including leadership training as part of the curriculum is especially important for Hispanic and other minority groups because leaders are needed in all aspects of our society. Culturally different children need to see culturally different leaders as role models. Our society must develop leadership talent from all sources.

Incorporate mentors into the curriculum. It is very important to incorporate mentors and role models into the program for gifted bilingual students, because mentors provide positive role models, exemplify possible career options, and offer personal and academic support (Baldwin, 1978; Dunham & Russo, 1983; Fitzgerald, 1973; Middlebrooks & Strong, 1982; Resources for Youth, 1980; VanTassel-Baska, Patton, & Prillaman, 1989). The vast majority of literature on mentorships concentrates on adult-child relationships in which the adult serves as the mentor and the child as the student. However, in an article by Wright and Borland (1992) another way of mentoring relationships is described which is particularly relevant to gifted bilingual students. It involves gifted adolescents serving as mentors to younger potentially gifted students. As Wright and Borland (1992) stated, the linking of a potentially gifted young child with an older academically gifted student from the same city and the same culture promises a number of benefits. The gifted adolescent is a living example of an intelligent person who has achieved academic success. Adolescent mentors can familiarize young potentially gifted children with the activities that lead to success in their area of expertise by guiding them in the classroom.

Mentor programs are valuable for both leadership training and career education. Career education, according to Bernal

(1976), is learning not only job skills but also how to make intelligent decisions as a result of concrete experiences with various jobs. Career education provides an opportunity to conceptualize what the work is about and what kind of work one can do and would most like to do. Career information can provide the gifted Hispanic student with a focus on future goals and plans. Hispanic students, particularly those who are poor, monolingual in Spanish, or female, need to be exposed to a wide variety of career options.

Emphasize counseling services as a central part of the program. Counseling must be offered to students with limited English proficiency in order to assist them in dealing with issues which are unique to their cultural adjustment. Other critical components of an exemplary counseling program include assisting all students to develop respect for cultural differences, and helping students develop a positive image of themselves and their environment. Students need to understand and incorporate into their self-concept the fact that they are gifted, and both students and parents need to know how to cope with these gifts and talents. Also, parent liaisons can assist in reducing barriers between the home and the school.

Involve the community and the parents in the program. The literature stresses the important relationship between early home influences and a young child's performance. What goes on at home, as well as parental attitudes and expectations toward education, are of vital importance in determining whether children succeed or fail in school. What parents do in their interactions with their children at home is the key determiner of students' success in school. In the words of Bempechat (1990) parents' behaviors with their children influence the children's cognitive and social development. Aspects of parental involvement in Hispanic families will be discussed in chapter 5.

In addition to parental involvement, community involvement should be stressed and should include various groups (e.g., public welfare program, charitable organizations, neighborhood centers, local business and industry, local museums, social service agencies, hospitals, and universities).

Programs for Gifted Bilingual Students in New York

Research findings support the fact that there is an evident lack of specialized programs for gifted bilingual children, even in states with high concentration of Hispanic students. Bermúdez et al. (1991) developed a combined multiple-choice and open-ended survey to examine the status of identification, placement, and instructional procedures for gifted and talented students from culturally and linguistically different groups. The survey was mailed to 500 gifted and talented coordinators from public school districts in five states with a high concentration of Hispanic students (Texas, California, Arizona, Colorado, and Florida). There were 268 respondents who provide the following information regarding programs for gifted students with limited English proficiency: Only 8.6 percent (23) of the total respondents (268) had any type of program to serve these students. Even though research has identified effective materials which differentiate the content of instruction to accommodate the needs of gifted students from culturally and linguistically different groups—for example, interdisciplinary courses, visual and performing arts experiences, focus on cultural values, focus on career education; and multicultural emphasis on the curriculum—only 8.7 percent (23) of those respondents who indicated an established program for this type of student reported the use of differentiated materials. In addition, 78 percent of the established programs follow a theoretically founded model of gifted education. Of these, 22.7 percent use Renzulli's Triad Model and 50 percent a combination. There were six missing responses, which could indicate, according to Bermúdez et al. (1991), the school's unawareness of theoretical and research foundations available for this area.

Evidently, these survey data indicate that there are very few programs, which are successful in instructing gifted and talented students from culturally and linguistically different groups, even in states with high Hispanic concentrations.

According to the U.S. Bureau of the Census (1997) 16.1 percent of the total U.S. Hispanic population reside in New York. Despite these numbers, currently in New York City there are only three programs that provide educational opportunities for gifted bilingual children: the Bilingual Bicultural Mini School, the Dual

Language Program for Gifted and Talented at P.S. 163, located in Community School District #3 in New York City, and the Discovery School for the Gifted, located in Community School District #6 in New York City.

The Bilingual Bicultural Mini School (BBMS), through the Emergency School Aid Act (ESAA), was founded in September 1973 and became the first bilingual bicultural elementary school in District #4. Located in East Harlem, the total population at the BBMS includes 550 students: 85 percent are Hispanic, 11 percent are African American, and 4 percent other. The BBMS services children that are Spanish dominant, English dominant, and intellectually gifted. Today the BBMS serves as a school of choice for limited English-proficient students as well as English-dominant students who are learning Spanish as a second language. The central mission is to provide truly bilingual and bicultural kindergarten through sixth grade curriculum, which retains the integrity and value of the children's cultural and linguistic heritage. At the BBMS they believe that the children's fluency in other languages and understanding many cultures represents an asset to be cultivated.

The emphasis of the instructional program is on the development of students' critical and creative thinking skills, regardless of their language dominance. The students are given opportunities to explore interests and extend an integrated curriculum by working on independent and cooperative projects. The Renzulli Enrichment Triad Model helps teachers plan and design such opportunities. In addition, collaborations with academic and cultural institutions such as El Museo del Barrio, the Central Park Conservancy, Mount Sinai Hospital, and Hunter College provide educational resources for the students.

The Dual Language Program for Gifted and Talented at P.S. 163 is located in New York City's Community School District #3, and, according to a brochure that describes the school, it is "a good place to learn, where a multi-ethnic staff and student population work together in a nurturing learning environment." The Dual Language Program for Gifted and Talented is one of five programs offered by the school. Each of the five programs has its own faculty, admission requirements, and curriculum. The Dual Language Program for Gifted and Talented serves children from kindergarten to fourth grade. According to a brochure describing the program, "it is open to both English and Spanish dominant students; it provides an opportunity to learn in two languages concurrently; and it encourages students to think critically and to solve problems creatively." This program is available only to students who have been accepted by District #3 to the Gifted and Talented Program. It is by parent request that the children are placed in the dual language program. The admission process to the Gifted and Talented Program requires an application, a teacher evaluation, and a standardized test (no fixed cut-off scores are required).

The Discovery School for the Gifted is a special two-way bilingual program for gifted children, housed in P.S. 98, a regular neighborhood school in New York City's Community School District #6. This special program has its own administration, faculty, admission requirements, and curriculum. According to a brochure that describes the school, "the goal in creating the Discovery School is to develop a supportive, educational setting where children can heighten their giftedness through a multicultural, two-way bilingual, discovery approach." The brochure continues describing the program as "collaborative and interdisciplinary. It nurtures the whole child. Teachers and paraprofessionals provide input to create meaningful experiences. They are familiarized with each child's capabilities and needs, and based on this information assign them stimulating and challenging work. The classroom and the community become laboratories for learning through trips that reinforce learning on a deeper level."

The program's brochure describes the curriculum framework as:

> Developmental, sensitive to the characteristics of young children as learners; multicultural, sensitive to the issues of diversity in the children's family traditions and their day-to-day experience; experiential because it incorporates manipulative materials and an active learning mode as frequently as possible; multidisciplinary since it integrates subject areas and uses a thematic approach to planning; language-rich in that it encourages the children to use language in the content of all learning activities; two-way bilingual because all children receive part of their instructional program in English and part in Spanish. The goal is complete bilingualism.

The admission process requires an application, a parent checklist, a teacher evaluation, a standardized test, and a student's writing sample. Admission to the Discovery School is based on a holistic assessment. Priority for admission is given first to children residing in the P.S. 98 zone.

Educational practices for gifted Hispanic students cannot simply be taken from a template and applied to any situation. Educators interested in providing quality programs for gifted Hispanic students must be willing to assess students' needs, as well as the political, economic, social, and educational issues in the institutional environment that will host the proposed educational service, and plan accordingly.

The shortage of specialized programs for gifted bilingual children is perplexing. Is there a lack of demand or need of such programs? Are there issues of efficiency of bilingual education involved? Bilingual education needs to be understood more deeply than simply as an issue of learning a second language. The fundamentals of dual language for curriculum and instruction reside in acquiring, developing, and maintaining the use of two languages because fluent bilingualism is an intellectual and cultural resource. Perhaps the need for more reliable evidence that bilingual programs produce students who are well educated in English and in the native language extends to the education of the gifted students as well. In addition, efforts to disseminate information regarding the availability, special characteristics, benefits, and advantages of bilingual programs, and specifically of special programs for gifted bilingual students should be considered a priority in any educational dialogue. Hispanic parents of potentially gifted children who need to make appropriate educational placement decisions are in need of this information.

Although the challenges of educating the gifted bilingual child are numerous, the potential benefits are many. An educational system that can meet the needs of this population can facilitate the development of a society that is enriched by the linguistic and cultural heritage of all citizens, participating on an equitable educational basis.

The Role of the Teacher in Educational
Service Delivery for Gifted Bilingual Students

In all educational programs, the teacher is the key to effective learning. It is the teacher who sets the environment which inspires or destroys self-confidence, encourages or suppresses interests, develops or neglects abilities, fosters or banishes creativity, stimulates or discourages critical thinking, and facilitates or frustrates achievement.

Teachers of gifted students have been studied from several perspectives: the characteristics needed to be effective teachers of gifted students (Ferrell, Kress, & Croft, 1988; Story, 1985); the characteristics of teachers most liked by the gifted students (Dorhout, 1983; Maddux, Samples-Lachman, & Cummings, 1985); the relationship between teachers of the gifted and regular classroom teachers (Meyers, 1984); the differences between experienced and new teachers of the gifted (Hanninen, 1988); and development and evaluation of training program models for teachers of the gifted (Clark, 1997; Kitano, 1982; Weiss & Gallagher, 1986).

Whether or not successful teachers of the gifted actually have unique abilities compared to other teachers is debatable. However, taken collectively they need to exhibit certain skills consistently. For example, teachers need to know and understand the cognitive, social, and emotional characteristics, needs, and problems found in gifted students. They need to develop a flexible, individualized, enriching curriculum appropriate to meeting the needs of the gifted students. They need to be able to teach higher order cognitive skills. They need to build self-respect and trust within the classroom, and be able to use a large number of strategies and skills to best serve the educational demands of gifted learners. They must provide role models for their students.

Teachers of the culturally and linguistically different gifted child would need yet additional understandings, dispositions, and skills to adapt to the different learning and motivational styles of students from these populations. These teachers would need to understand the students' cultural values and linguistic characteristics and translate such understanding into classroom practices; foster sociolinguistic tolerance among pupils; learn to identify and build upon the strengths these students demonstrate; and very importantly, believe in the student and believe in the program.

When addressing the needs of students with limited English proficiency, teachers need to be knowledgeable of the stages involved in first and second language acquisition in order to support the gifted student's ongoing development in both languages.

Teachers should not confuse limitations in the second language with limitations in academic cognitive ability. Teachers often have low curriculum expectations for students with limited English proficiency because they perceive these students as having inadequate skill development due to their being in a transitional stage between their first and second language.

It is important and certainly beneficial that the teachers be proficient in the student's language, especially if the students are given the opportunity to pursue their interests in their first language. In addition, well-prepared bilingual teachers and staff who speak the native language and understand the home culture appear to have the most direct influence on the students' self-esteem, as well as on the cognitive and affective growth of students whose primary language is other than English.

Does training teachers improve the education of gifted students from culturally and linguistically different groups? The balance of evidence indicates that it definitively does. Trained teachers can better identify and instruct gifted children than untrained teachers (Bermúdez & Rakow, 1990; Clark, 1997; Passow, 1982; Shore & Kaizer, 1989; Valencia, 1985). Identification procedures for gifted bilingual students must take into account those behaviors, linguistic and cultural, that could mask giftedness. Such behaviors, according to Bermúdez and Rakow (1990), include nonverbal cues which often do not transfer from one cultural context to another. This lack of knowledge results in false interpretations of the information and subsequent improper identification, placement, and instruction of learners in need of specialized educational programs.

Clark (1990) stresses that a good teacher-training program should incorporate developing the teacher's cognitive academic language proficiency and cultural sensitivity, along with the competencies necessary for implementing effective dual-language programs. In addition, García (1992) points out that in any discussion of a professional training program for second-language-learner students, it is important to include credentialing and professional assessment issues.

According to Márquez and Sawyer (1994), cultural awareness can be attained through formal training or through experiences. They strongly promote the concept of students teaching teachers about their culture through informal sharing experiences. The sharing of personal experiences will enhance the opportunity for students and educators to become more familiar with different cultural values and lifestyles. The key to in-service training should be to sensitize teachers not only to the characteristics of culturally and linguistically different learners but also, and perhaps more importantly, to the rights of these students to be what they are—gifted and different.

❧

Chapter Five

Involvement of Hispanic Parents in the Education of Their Gifted Child

Family involvement has become a popular concept for educators, as they increasingly recognize the benefits that result from engaging families in their children's education within and outside the classroom. Although models of family involvement are available (Epstein, 1995), their implementation can be difficult. Families do not share the same backgrounds and interests, skills and educational attainment, priorities and needs. Family schedules do not allow for uniform activities. Families embrace children with different needs, abilities, and potential. Being the parent of a child with unusual talents or potential brings some risks, challenges, and joys. Some parents will deny their children's special abilities in an attempt to keep them "normal" and "well-adjusted." Some others will magnify their children's abilities and put excessive pressure on them for high achievement in all areas. And some others will adopt an attitude of indifference toward their children's special abilities. By building a partnership with the school and becoming part of their children's education and development, parents will be able to develop realistic expectations regarding their children's abilities and create a supportive learning environment at home. Partnerships between parents and school create better programs and opportunities for students (Epstein, 1995).

Contrasting Patterns of Involvement
in Low-Income and High-Income Parents

The research literature supports the fact that involving Hispanic and low-income parents in their children's education is by no means an easy task. Lareau (1987) conducted interviews with parents, teachers, and principals of first and second grade students in low and middle socioeconomic status (SES) schools. There were no SES differences in concern about their children's education. However, low SES parents had greater doubts about their efficacy to help their children in school. Middle SES parents viewed the education of their children as a shared responsibility between parents and school, while low SES parents tended to see it as exclusively the responsibility of the school. Lower SES parents were reluctant to try to help their children at home for fear that they might mislead them. Lareau concluded that lower SES parents' inferior education and low prestige made them more dependent on educators to know what is best for their children.

Similar findings were reported by Delgado-Gaitán's study (1994) in which the importance of the role of Mexican parents in their children's education was studied. Mexican parents who have less formal schooling and limited knowledge of and information about the schooling process were less involved in school matters and felt more powerless in working with their children in school assignments. Delgado-Gaitán's study emphasizes formal education as a significant factor for parental involvement. She suggests that parents with less formal education can be empowered by giving them access to knowledge of how the system works.

McLaughlin and Shields (1987) suggested that involvement of low-income and poorly educated parents should be an educational priority for two reasons: (a) Those parents want to become involved in their children's education; and (b) Demographic trends indicate that children increasingly are coming from nontraditional families. McLaughlin and Shields feel that parent involvement does not work if mandated; professionals need to support the idea that the inclusion of low-income parents in education is beneficial to the children, the educational process, and the school.

When dealing, specifically, with the involvement of Hispanic parents of potentially gifted children, additional matters need to be considered. It is worth emphasizing that Hispanics include people from numerous and very different national backgrounds. The range of Hispanics varies from those who are new immigrants from rural villages to those who have had families in the United States for generations; from those who live in the Spanish-speaking "barrios" to those who live in the suburbs. Linguistically, the Hispanic population ranges from those who are monolingual Spanish or English speakers to those who are fully bilingual. These differences can affect the relationship between the school and the parents.

Furthermore, it is important to be aware of the fact that since gifted education is not as fully developed throughout the Spanish-speaking countries as it is in the United States, it is possible that none of the parents have heard of it in the home countries and are therefore unaware of the advantages and benefits of a program for gifted children. These parents will become supportive and involved only if they understand the child's gifts and talents, and if they understand the opportunities available to the gifted in our society. Furthermore, they are more likely to assist their children and contribute to the special program if they do not see the program as elitist or as threatening. If parents believe in the idea that the gifted program will cause their children to respect them less, or if they are frightened that they will not be able to provide academic and educational support, or that the program will alienate the child from them, parents will likely resist a gifted program.

Getting parents to participate—even at a minimal level—helps overcome many parents' initial feelings of anxiety about becoming involved in school activities or acting as an advocate for their children in the educational system. Often, this apprehensiveness arises from feelings of alienation from a system they do not readily understand. Additionally, many Hispanic parents will feel uncomfortable within the school environment because of lack of communication, inaccessibility of the meeting sites, lack of child care, negative past experiences with schools, insensitivity, and hostility on the part of school personnel (Bermúdez, 1994). School personnel need to make every possible effort to provide flexible and varied opportunities for parents to become involved. The school's personnel effort can make an alien system more comprehensible.

According to Bermúdez (1994), Inger (1992), and Nazzaro and Portuondo (1981), parental involvement can be encouraged if (a) meetings are scheduled at times and in places that are accessible; (b) interpreters are available; (c) a warm and caring environment is created; (d) ample information is provided; (e) child care is provided; (f) materials in the parents' language are provided; and (g) transportation is provided. Most importantly, educators must be committed to work with parents as partners in the educational process.

The portraits presented in this book illustrate the impact of parental involvement in the education of Hispanic children with high potential. Because of the retrospective nature of the portraits, it was possible to discern patterns of behavior over a period of time and the effects these behaviors had on the individuals involved. The parents of the three children, especially the mothers, had to be advocates for their children to get the educational services they needed. The mothers had to learn to trust and work with people from the special programs to discover a world they were not aware of. They had to learn the workings of an unfamiliar educational system and extend the learning experience to home. The goal of providing their children with the best educational opportunities possible served as anchor to several patterns of behavior.

Oscar's mother always fought for a good education for her children. She trusted Oscar's abilities and talent and had a great deal of confidence in him. She constantly encouraged him to succeed and to work hard in school. Overlooking her poor English skills, Oscar's mother became extremely involved in Oscar's school, volunteering in the classroom and learning the workings and specifics of the educational setting. Her strong and positive presence made a difference in Oscar's educational career. She was always helping him, always bringing the best support material home and always caring for Oscar's best interests. Oscar's academic excellence and high performance are the result, in part, of such a strong support system. This concurs with Bempechat's (1990) and Carrasquillo's (1991) assertion that what parents do in their interactions with their children at home is the key determiner of students' success in school.

Gaby's mother case comes from a family of professionals and hardworking people. She understands and values the role of a good and solid education. She always wanted to see her daughters in a good school, with a solid education, and eventually with a good job. Gaby's mother has always been very clear on these goals and, as the case study illustrates, she was ready to make any sacrifice, even staying in New York City away from her family.

Nonetheless, Gaby's mother's involvement and communication with the school was not as strong and interactive as in Oscar's mother case. At the beginning of Gaby's school, her involvement was very limited and marginal. It was not until third grade, when Gaby's academic difficulties began, that she became somewhat more involved. She started to talk to the teacher and visited the classroom occasionally in order to understand her daughter's difficulties. Gaby's elementary school takes a progressive approach to education, and this was difficult for Gaby's mother to understand. Gaby's mother never abandoned her advocacy role. She just did not become very aggressive in helping Gaby overcome her academic difficulties. Perhaps Gaby's mother felt powerless or lacked the knowledge base necessary to identify her daughter's difficulties earlier. She just did not understand the course of Gaby's performance and did not know what to do.

A study done by Delgado-Gaitán (1994) regarding the role of Hispanic parents in their children's education suggests that families with less formal schooling have greater feelings of powerlessness regarding what action to take in their children's education. This emphasizes formal education as a significant factor in parental involvement. Gaby's mother could have been empowered by gaining her access to knowledge of learning difficulties and patterns of behavior, just as Project Synergy empowered her, through several workshops, on the workings of the school system and how to advocate for her daughter. Enhancing parenting skills should be part of any parent support group activity.

Unlike Oscar's and Gaby's mother, Tina's mother's advocacy, support, and involvement went beyond providing Tina with the best educational opportunities possible. Her involvement was much more interactive and ambitious. As Tina grows up, not only is her mother more involved and dedicated, but the message regarding the importance of being educated are stronger and more direct.

Tina's mother has always reinforced what she learns in school by reading, going to field trips, watching movies, and sometimes talking to experts in the topic. This reinforces the mother's commitment to education and sets an example of involvement. For this mother, education is the key to success. She has always encouraged Tina to reach for more, to be ambitious regarding knowledge and experience.

Creating a supportive learning environment at home, encouraging positive attitudes toward schooling, and having high expectations for the children's accomplishments raises student achievement. To a different extent this is true for all three children portrayed in the case studies.

❦

Part III

Portraits

The following three portraits are the result of a qualitative, retro-spective case study approach. Each one of the portraits illustrates the educational experiences of gifted bilingual students who were identified as potentially gifted by either Project Synergy Preschool and placed in special educational programs. The portraits focus on the impact of either Project Synergy or Project Synergy Preschool on the educational placement decision of these three Hispanic families, and on the school adjustment of the students in their re-spective schools.

The goal of presenting the case studies is to provide the reader with the insight and understanding into the educational experi-ences of three Hispanic students identified as potentially gifted living in New York City. Each story is unique, and one should not attempt to generalize from it to the entire Hispanic population living in this country.

Because a deeper understanding of specific issues and problems related to a particular practice was sought in each portrait, a qualitative, retrospective case study approach was used. The field of education has turned to case study research to explore and address problems in which in depth understanding, discovery and interpretation are sought in order to improve practice (Merriam, 1988). As a consequence, several research reports, journal articles, and books have been published recognizing the benefits, uses, and advantages of utilizing a case study approach for better understanding of certain aspects of educational practice. This book is one such source.

Different sources of date were used for these retrospective case studies. For instance, the students, their parents, and their teachers were interviewed on several occasions and at different sites; observations at the various educational settings were done; and grade transcripts were reviewed.

Each case study begins with a description of the student, including background, family composition, community, educational level, occupation, language dominance, and other information that was deemed important. Next comes information concerning the students' educational experiences; the impact of being identified as a student with high academic potential as well as the impact of Project Synergy on the educational placement decision; and finally the students' adjustment to their respective schools. A glimpse of the participants' voices is embedded in the narrative to preserve the authenticity of the experience without analysis or interpretation.

✣

Chapter Six

Oscar: "Being Hispanic Is a Gift That Does Not Need a Special Program in Order to Be Nurtured"

Background

Oscar is a well-built, cooperative youngster who will turn 16 in the summer of 2001. He appears, at first, to be quite shy, but when relaxed, he speaks easily, revealing fluency both in Spanish and English.

Oscar is the second of three children of an intact family living in a predominantly low-income community in New York City's Upper West Side. His sister is 15 years older. He states that she has always been a great source of love and support for him and that she is "a positive role model for me." Oscar's younger brother turned 12 in October of 2000 and it is reported that, although they have very different personalities, they have a good relationship.

Oscar was born in New York City; both the pregnancy and birth were normal. His mother stated that since Oscar was born everything was different, not only because he was born 15 years after his sister, but also because he was a boy. Since Oscar was born "he has been very special." He was always very alert and was a curious and content baby.

Oscar's father was born and raised in Ecuador, South America. He worked as an accountant in Ecuador, but when the family moved to New York in 1969, he had to find other jobs because he had neither fluency in English nor the college credits to work as

an accountant in this country. He is currently working in the as-
bestos removal industry. Oscar's father has always supported and
he has been involved in his children's education; he works with
them and he encourages them to "read a lot, to make their homework, and to be good students." His great mathematical ability
allows him to help the children with math, and it is stated that
"he always likes to challenge the children with mathematical
questions, always demanding good answers every time he asks a
question."

Oscar's mother is an enthusiastic and cooperative woman devoted to giving her children the best education possible. She was
also born and raised in Ecuador, where she worked in a well-
known bank in Guayaquil. She completed high school in Ecuador
but she never got the diploma. Recently she took the exam for the
GED in a New York City college and earned her diploma. When
she first arrived in the United States, Oscar's mother worked as a
full-time seamstress in a factory, where her ambition and drive for
self-improvement led to her becoming the sewing-room's supervi-
sor in a short period of time. Besides taking an English as a Second Language course, she is currently taking a course on
advanced pastry and cake decoration. She is also doing house-
keeping jobs, and sometimes she bakes cakes for sale. She would
love to study and become a "well known chef."

Oscar's mother has always demonstrated a strong commitment to and advocacy for Oscar's education. She states that she is
always "trying to get the best books for him, to be an active par-
ticipant in his school, to help him with homework when needed, to
read with him, and to learn with him." For her, the most important aspect in her children's education is reading:

> *Ellos necesitan leer bastante. Quiero que les guste la lectura porque es
> la llave del mundo, uno puede estar encerrado en este cuarto y saber
> todo lo que está pasando en el mundo simplemente leyendo.*

> They need to read a lot. I want them to like reading because it is the
> key to the world; one can be locked in this room and know what is
> happening in the rest of the world by merely reading.

Oscar senses this passion, and he reports an interest and joy
for reading, particularly real-life stories.

Most of Oscar's extended family lives in Ecuador, and, although he does not get a chance to visit them very often, he is very aware of his family and tries to stay in touch with them by phone or letters. He is hoping to visit them next summer.

I met Oscar and his family for the first time when I was working as a consultant teacher for Project Synergy, a federally funded project at Teachers College, Columbia University, whose purpose is to identify potentially gifted economically disadvantaged young children and to provide transitional services to the children, their families, and their teachers. By the time I started with the project, Oscar had already been identified by the project as potentially gifted. He was part of the project's first cohort of 18 children.

Signs of Precocity and Development of Talent Potential

According to Oscar's mother, he was a very curious, alert, and happy baby. Oscar's first language was Spanish, which he spoke before the age of two. He was always asking questions, expecting detailed answers. His drawing ability has been evident since he was a little boy. When he was 2 years old he started to draw lines resembling cars and buses, and soon, when he turned 3, these drawings became magnificent samples full of details and color.

When Oscar was 3 years old, he and his mother moved back to Ecuador (his sister was living there with the grandparents) for two years. He completed a year of nursery and soon began to recognize all the letters, numbers, colors, and shapes. In fact, his mother stated that the teacher in Ecuador from very early on recognized Oscar's talent but did not do much to nurture that potential. She recalls the teacher saying that Oscar "is very, very smart but I do not know how to work with him." Due to family circumstances, they had to move back to New York in the summer of 1990.

In August of the same year, not knowing about educational options and school placements, Oscar's mother registered him in the public school of their neighborhood. However, because they missed the registration period, their neighborhood school could not take him so he was transferred to another public school where more spaces were available, the kindergarten bilingual program at the Public School 149/207 in Community School District #3 in Central Harlem. This elementary school serves an economically disadvantaged minority population that is three-quarters African American and one-quarter Hispanic. P.S. 149/207 was classified as a School Under Registration Review, meaning that, as a result of a history of poor student achievement, the school is being monitored by the State of New York and may be decertified and closed should student performance not improve. New York City elementary schools are ranked annually according to the number of students who score at grade level on the Degrees of Reading Power Test. In the 1992–1993 academic year, P.S. 149/207 ranked 617th out of 625 New York City public elementary schools, with only 14.1 percent of its students reading on grade level (Borland, 1994). Reading scores have improved since then, and by the 1995–1996 academic year, the school was no longer considered under registration review.

Oscar began in the bilingual kindergarten with a positive attitude. According to his mother, "he did not have any trouble adjusting to the school and the country in general." She was very happy that, even though the program was "bilingual," most of the day the teachers and students spoke Spanish due to the fact that none of the kids in the classroom understood or spoke a word of English. Oscar demonstrated leadership ability from the beginning. He was always organizing the games and activities during recess and was always the first on line. Also, even though his academic mastery gave him an academic advantage over the rest of the class, he always helped other children and felt like *"un chico grande encargado de todo"* (like a big kid in charge of everything).

At the end of the school year, together with his kindergarten certificate, Oscar's parents received a letter from the principal notifying them "about a new program for the kindergarten children called 'Project Synergy,' funded by the Federal government to find children with high academic promise and provide enrichment services for them." Oscar was selected as one of those children to receive a full scholarship to Project Synergy's enrichment program beginning in the summer of 1991.

One of Project Synergy's goals is ultimately to place the identified students in appropriate educational settings so their academic, social, and emotional needs will be met. However, because Synergy's identification was done at the end of the kindergarten school year, Oscar had to stay one more year at P.S. 149/207 before being able to join a different program.

Since Oscar was staying at the same school for first grade, Oscar's kindergarten teacher suggested to Oscar's parents that he would be placed in the all-English first grade because "his ability and potential are so great that he does not need to be in a bilingual program." They took the offer, thinking that this was best for Oscar and that he would benefit from an all-English class as opposed to a bilingual program.

Oscar began first grade and, according to his mother, the teacher was "nice." However, his lack of English proficiency resulted in some academic difficulties. Oscar's mother was very frustrated and disappointed because neither she nor any other member of the family could help Oscar with school homework because none of them spoke English and because Oscar's academic achievement was not as good as in the kindergarten year. Oscar's mother requested a teacher conference to express her concerns. The teacher never questioned Oscar's abilities. She said that it was just a "matter of time, and he'll be fully bilingual." But Oscar became a shy, quiet, and not very social child. He had difficulty understanding the teacher and the children and vice versa. The following excerpt from a conversation with Oscar and his mother reveals this dissatisfaction.

OSCAR: Yo recuerdo que cuando me pasaron a otro salón y ya no estaba con Ms. Y me puse muy afligido. Yo estaba solo, no tenía amigos, como que yo estaba metido en mí y me alejaba mucho de todos. También recuerdo que como yo no sabía inglés yo no entendía nada de lo que me hablaban y me costó trabajo estar ahí. Recuerdo pasar el tiempo jugando....
MADRE: Nosotros no sabíamos qué hacer, y como la maestra nos sugirió que lo cambiaran al salón de puro inglés por sus buenas calificaciones entonces lo cambiamos, pero lo veía a él mas retraído y con pocos amigos.
OSCAR: I recalled that when I was placed in another room, not with Ms. Y, I was very distressed. I was alone, I didn't have friends, as though I was on my own, and I pulled away from all the kids. Besides, since I didn't speak English, I did not understand what every-

body said and it was hard for me. I recalled spending time just playing....

MOTHER: We really did not know what to do, and since the teacher suggested that he'd be in an all-English classroom because of his grades, we accepted. But I noticed he became lonely and with very few friends.

The whole picture turned brighter once Oscar started a tutoring program at the Child Study Center at Teachers College, Columbia University, in the fall of 1991. Despite the fact that this tutoring program at the Child Study Center was not part of Project Synergy, Oscar was referred to it by Project Synergy so he could improve his English skills.

Even though Oscar's knowledge and usage of English vocabulary were still limited at that point, he made great progress in reading and he was invited back to the Child Study Center for the spring semester of 1992. Oscar himself perceived a big change in his social life:

> *Cuando me dieron la tutoría yo ya sabía más inglés y ya empecé a hacer más amigos.*

> When I started with the tutoring program I learned some English and I made new friends.

During the spring semester at the Child Study Center, reading was not the only area addressed. Mathematics was introduced, but as an exercise with basic number facts, not as a remediation program. Oscar progressed significantly in the tutoring program. His usage of English vocabulary improved. Both the tutor and the Director of the Child Study Center described Oscar as "enthusiastic, creative and strong minded." They have also consistently characterized Oscar as "cooperative, quick to make connections and understand concepts, and motivated."

Oscar completed his tutoring program at the Child Study Center as well as his first grade year at P.S. 149/207 with a positive attitude and a small group of friends. Now it was time to be transferred to a different school environment. So, at Synergy's suggestion, Oscar, together with four other children who were also selected to participate in the project, requested to transfer to a special program designed exclusively for children identified as gifted. After exploring and visiting several educational options, under Synergy's supervision, Oscar's parents decided to register him at the New York City Laboratory School for Gifted Education in Community School District #2 for the fall of 1992. Oscar's mother explains what made them choose the Lab School.

A mí las cosas que mas me gustaron de la escuela fueron que es pequeña, no quería yo una escuela que tenga sobrepoblación de estudiantes; también me llamó mucho la atención la forma en la que los chicos se llevaban con D (la directora) y con todos los maestros en general, les hablaban por el primer nombre y no con el "Ms" como en P.S. 149; D conocía a todos los alumnos por nombre y eso me gustó. También me gustó mucho el vecindario de la escuela.

Yo vi que el Lab School era diferente porque aqui sí hay una mezcla de culturas; en la escuela 149 no había mezcla, eran solamente Hispanos y morenos. Es importante que los hijos conozcan de todas las culturas y las respeten. Que se junten con todo tipo de gente.

Yo buscaba una escuela que le brinde las mejores oportunidades a Oscar, que no tenga un ambiente aburrido, que los muchachos sean activos, que hagan cosas constantemente. Yo vi que en el Lab School ese ambiente existía y me pareció muy bien.

The things I liked most about the school were that is a small school; I didn't want a school overpopulated with students. I also noted the way the kids got along with D (the principal) and with all the teachers in general. They addressed them using their first name and not "Ms" as in P.S. 149; D knew all the children's names, and we liked that; we also liked the neighborhood where the school was located.

I saw that the Lab School was different because there is a mix of cultures; in P.S. 149 there was no mix, there were only Blacks and Hispanics. It is important that our children learn and respect all different cultures, that they be surrounded by all kinds of people.

I was looking for a school that will give him the best opportunities, where the environment is not boring, where the children are active, doing things constantly. I saw that environment at the Lab School, and I liked it.

Oscar attended the Lab School from second to fifth grades.

The Laboratory School for Gifted Children

This school is housed in a regular neighborhood school on New York City's Upper East Side. This special program has its own administration, faculty, admission requirements, and curriculum. The Lab School operates on the premise that gifted education need not be elitist. The population is ethnically and socioeconomically diverse, serving students ranging from those in the upper middle class to those receiving free breakfasts and lunches. It uses flexible or mixed-aged class groupings serving ages 4 through 10–11 (kindergarten through fifth grade). The admission process requires a group tour before application is made. The tour is followed by an explanation of the school's philosophy and a question-and-answer session. Parents are then given an application. The application requires a skill checklist, a teacher evaluation, and a 60-minute student observation. There are no fixed cut-off scores on standardized tests.

Oscar started second grade at the Lab School, which was, by no means, an easy one. Oscar had difficulties adjusting to the new environment, resulting in emotional, academic, and social distress. According to Oscar's mother, the transition to this new school was somehow traumatic. The following excerpt describes Oscar's mother emotions of that beginning:

Fue un cambio muy drástico en cuanto a escuelas. Para mí fue muy difícil también. Yo pienso que la maestra que le tocó en ese segundo grado no es la mas apropiada para un segundo grado, bueno esto lo sé ahora que ya pasaron varios años, no lo entendía yo así al principio. Con su experiencia y su carácter a ella le va mucho mejor ser maestra de grados superiores, quinto, sexto, y eso le chocó mucho al principio a Oscar, ella era bien fuerte de carácter. A mí también me chocó mucho ese primer año porque yo quería acercarme a ella para preguntarle cómo iba él en la escuela porque yo tenía temor de que él no estuviera haciendo bien las cosas, yo inclusive le mandé en varias ocasiones una nota pidiéndole una entrevista para hablar con ella porque a mí se me había dicho que eso se podía hacer. Yo estaba consciente de que había ciertas regulaciones dentro de la escuela como que yo no podía ir a cualquier hora para pedir información y yo siempre traté de que no hubieran problemas, de no causar problemas. Yo me acuerdo de que una de las últimas notas la mandé antes de salir de vacaciones, entonces ella me devolvió la nota, sin escribir nada, y en boca de Oscar me decía que no tenía tiempo. Me sentí muy mal, yo no me pude acercar a la escuela. Solamente iba a recoger las calificaciones de Oscar.

It was a very drastic change concerning schools. It was hard for me, too. I feel that the teacher he had in second grade was not the most appropriate one for a second grade class. Well, now I know this, after many years have elapsed. At the beginning I didn't understand it this way. With her experience and personality, she would be better off teaching in higher grades, fifth, sixth. At the beginning Oscar hated it; she had a very strong personality. I also hated that first year. I wanted to approach her to ask her how was he doing in school because I was afraid that he wasn't doing things properly, I even sent her a note several times requesting an interview to speak with her because I had been told that you could do that. I was aware that there were certain regulations in school that I couldn't go at any time to ask for information, and I always tried to avoid problems, not to cause any problem.

I recall that one of the last notes I sent it before the break, she returned the same piece of paper, without writing anything on it, Oscar gave me the message that she didn't have time. I felt very bad; I was unable to approach the school during that first year! I only went to school when I was told to pick up Oscar's grades.

This frustration and lack of communication with the school was also shared and experienced by Oscar himself.

Bueno…yo me acuerdo que para mí fué difícil al principio…. En el Lab School como que todo era muy estricto, si te movías o hacías algo ya te estaban gritando y llamando la atención, eso me chocó, de estar en un sitio tranquilo donde nadie te grita a estar en un lugar donde eran puros gritos y todo el mundo me empezaba a atacar.

Lo que a mí mas me pone bravo es que alguien me grite y no soportaba que C (la maestra) me gritara a cada momento. Yo trataba de entender lo que ella decía pero a veces como ella explicaba las cosas yo no le podía entender y es por eso que preguntaba. Si mi inglés hubiera estado mas fuerte
yo no preguntaría tanto.

Well…I remember it was hard at the beginning…. At the Lab School it wasn't, it was like everything was stricter, if you moved or did something they yelled and scolded you, I hated that, from being in a quiet place where no one yells at you to be in a place where you just heard shouts and everyone attacked me.

What really makes me mad is someone yelling at me and I couldn't stand C (the teacher) yelling at me all the time. I tried to understand what she was saying but at times I couldn't understand her when she explained things and that is why I asked. Had my English proficiency been better, I wouldn't ask so much.

Academically speaking, Oscar also had to make some adjustments. He came from a school where, according to him, everything was easy and not very challenging. Also, as reflected in the previous descriptions, P.S. 149/207 was a more relaxed and less noisy environment. In contrast, the Lab School was a more demanding and challenging academic setting. Oscar had to read and write quite a bit (in English), homework and projects were constantly in his backpack, and class assignments were sometimes confusing and misunderstood. In the classroom, the noise and activity were usually at a high level. Children talked in loud voices, they constantly moved throughout the room, and, as a consequence, the volume of the teacher's directions and warnings had to be raised as well.

This new and stressful climate brought Oscar unhappiness and a desire to return to P.S. 149/207. However, he never insisted or pressured his parents to be relocated back to his old public school. In the spring of 1993 Oscar received the citywide reading and math tests. The percentile rank for the reading test was 61. Both Oscar and his parents were very disappointed by this score. They did not know if it was a matter of his lack of English proficiency, a lack of some skills that he did not have when he came to the Lab School that he should have had, or maybe the stressful classroom environment that resulted in, according to the mother, *"no muy buen resultado"* ("not a very good score"). Oscar's parents knew that he was capable of doing much better. Although it was difficult for Oscar's mother to understand the meaning of and find a convincing explanation for this "average" score, she did understand that with her help Oscar could progress and improve this score. The summer seemed to be a good time to do it. She bought a Spanish-English dictionary, a couple of new books, and together they started to read and to write brief book reports so Oscar could improve his reading and writing skills. Oscar himself described it as a busy and productive summer.

On the other hand, the math scores obtained on the brand new California Achievement Test (CAT-5) were much more encouraging for Oscar and his family. The reported percentile rank for the math test was 82. Oscar's performance on this test showed mastery in numeration, number theory, data interpretation, pre-algebra, and geometry. This math score can be accounted for Oscar's father involvement with math homework. Oscar's father was an accountant in Ecuador and, according to Oscar's mother, he has great mathematical ability.

These unfortunate academic and emotional circumstances resulted in social consequences as well. Oscar was not a very popular kid. His only friend was D, a boy also identified by Project Synergy. All of a sudden, Oscar decided that it was time to interact more with other children and expand his friendship relationships. He chose to become the class clown, showing off, joking, and fooling around in an effort to be accepted and to gain favorable attention.

Oscar did not gain any more friends or lasting relationships with his silly behavior. At home he constantly complained that he did not have any friends and that during recess time he had to be by himself. So his family, in an attempt to help Oscar expand his social interactions, came up with an idea:

MADRE: Oscar se quejaba de que no podía hacer amigos, que durante el recreo no jugaba con nadie y entonces se pensó que él llevara una pelota de soccer y asi todos los otros niños iban a venir a jugar con él.

OSCAR: Ah si, yo llevaba mi soccer ball y durante el recreo siempre jugabamos y así empecé a relacionarme con los otros niños. Yo todavía era amigo de D pero como él no es nada tímido él si hizo otros amigos y pues yo también y ya no estábamos todo el tiempo juntos como al principio.

MOTHER: Oscar complained he couldn't make friends, that during recess he didn't have anybody to play with so then we thought that if he took a soccer ball to school then the other kids would play with him.

OSCAR: Oh, yes, I started to take my soccer ball and we always played during recess and that is how I started to relate with the other children. I was still D's friend, but since he isn't shy at all, he did make other friends and so did I and we weren't together all the time, as we were early on.

According to Oscar and his mother, this idea turned out to be quite successful. It provided him with an opportunity for developing friendly relations. The support and encouragement he received from his family as well as the remarkable improvement in his

English skills helped him successfully complete that first year in a new and challenging environment.

Third Grade

Third grade represented a quite different experience for Oscar and his family at the Lab School. Oscar's parents had anticipated that since his early academic, social, and emotional difficulties had lessened by the end of last year, third grade could be a much better year. They were not prepared, however, for what they consider to be a total turnaround in his attitude and behavior. Oscar's mother described what happened during that third grade year.

> *Eso fue un cambio super drástico. Ahí ya tenían tercero y cuarto grado juntos y le toca una suavidad de maestra. Oscar estaba encantado con ella, creo que hasta hoy en día sigue enamorado de ella! Bueno imagínese el cambio tan drástico, primero le toca C de maestra que es tremendamente estricta y luego de golpe le ponen a esta maestra que era una dulzura y super suave y pues Oscar tomó ventaja de esto y empezó a tener muchos problemas serios de conducta. Toda la tensión que él tenía acumulada de estar con C y en la escuela nueva, la sacó con esta maestra que se llamaba L. Sus problemas de conducta se fueron haciendo cada vez mas grandes, se ponía muy malcreado en el salón, le decía constantemente a L que todo lo que ella le enseñaba él ya lo sabía y que no lo necesitaba saber de nuevo, entonces hubo muchas quejas hasta que un día me mandaron llamar y eso fué para mí un choque tremendo porque Oscar siempre ha sido muy bien portado y respetuoso, no lo podía yo creer que él estaba haciendo esas cosas.*

That was a drastic change. There they had third and fourth grades together, and they got a sweet, calm teacher. Oscar was very happy; to this day I think he is still in love with her! Just imagine what a drastic change. First he had C who was terribly strict, and then suddenly, he has this teacher who is so sweet and great. Well Oscar took advantage of this and began to have behavioral problems. All the stress he has accumulated after being with C came out with this teacher whose name was L. Oscar's behavioral problems increased. He was really misbehaving in the classroom. He said he knew everything that L was going to teach him and that he didn't need to know it again. Then there were many complaints until one day they called me, and that was a terrible shock for me, because he always behaved and was very respectful. I couldn't believe he was doing those things.

Oscar himself could not justify his new attitude. He just wanted to test the limits and see the reaction, and even though he knew this was not an acceptable behavior, he could not prevent himself from acting like that. He recognized that with L he was acting as he did in Public School 149/207 because *"en la 149 me parecía todo muy fácil"* ("everything was easy in P.S. 149").

Given these new and unexpected circumstances, Oscar, his mother, the teacher, and the Director got together to develop an immediate plan to remedy the situation:

> *MADRE: Entre todos llegamos a un acuerdo que era que cada viernes Oscar tenía que traer a la casa un reporte de cómo se había portado toda la semana, Oscar mismo hizo la hoja en la computadora...*
> *OSCAR: Si, yo lo puse en la computadora y era mi propio reporte, mi propio registro en donde la letra A era muy bien, la letra B era regular y la letra C era que caí por completo, entonces yo ponía los días de la semana y L (la maestra) me ponía la letra de cada día.*
> *MADRE: Al final de la semana si su conducta estaba bien entonces tenía un premio el fin de semana, como un paseo o algo que él quisiera hacer hasta que él solito supiera como debería comportarse.*

> MOTHER: We all reached an agreement in which he had to bring home a report on Friday saying how he had behaved during the week.
> OSCAR: Yes, I entered it into the computer and it was my own report, my own record, where A meant very good, B was fair and C meant to fail completely. So I put all the days of the week and L (the teacher) wrote the letter every day.
> MOTHER: At the end of the week if he behaved well, then he got a prize in the weekend, like a special activity or something else he wanted to do, until he knew for himself how to behave.

This plan proved to be a very good one. In a matter of weeks Oscar's behavior returned to a more acceptable course. Oscar's parents often praised and showed appreciation for his performance. Although they were concerned about his drastic change, they never pressured him. They trusted him and had confidence that this unexpected attitude would not last for long, that it was just a way of releasing old frustration and unhappiness.

Even though Oscar felt he was having a good year and that his misbehavior was not causing him any trouble on his academic performance, the citywide math and reading tests proved the opposite. The percentile rank for the math test was 65, and for the reading test it was 49, both significantly lower than previous years. Both Oscar and his family were very disappointed, and it was not until then that they realized that although L was a sweet, imaginative, and energetic teacher, she did not do much academically for Oscar.

By the end of third grade Oscar's self-esteem and self-confidence were much more positive. His English skills were stronger, his group of friends was bigger, his mother was very involved in the school, people in the school knew them better, their presence could be felt, and everybody started to make them feel part of the family. This was a good sign for the upcoming year.

Fourth Grade

By the time Oscar had reached fourth grade, he had developed a more solid sense of his abilities and was feeling more self-confident. He states that *"en ese momento yo ya me sentía muy bien en la escuela, estaba yo cómodo ahí"* ("by that time I felt okay in that school; I was comfortable"). Although Oscar acknowledged having been a "special kid" since he was in kindergarten, these special abilities and talent now played a predominant role in his functioning or in the way he viewed himself and is viewed by his family.

> *Yo ahora me doy cuenta de que capto las cosas muy rápido. No me gusta repetir las cosas que ya sé hacer. Para mí, me dicen algo, o leo las instrucciones y ya me pongo a trabajar inmediatamente, me distrae y me aburre escuchar lo mismo varias veces. Cuando acabo me gusta empezar otra cosa rápido porque si no comienzo a jugar. Yo hice muchos mas amigos. Conoces cada vez a más gente y tambien como veían que yo captaba todo rápido y entendía todo me empezaron a buscar muchos niños para que los ayude con la escuela y yo les explicaba a todos y así hice muchos amigos.*

Now I am aware that I grasp everything very fast. I don't like to repeat the things I already know how to do. They tell me something or

I read the instructions and I start to work immediately. I get distracted or bored listening to the same things several times. When I'm done, I like to begin something else fast because otherwise I start to play. I made a lot of more friends. You meet a lot of people, and also they saw how fast I grasped and understood everything. Many kids started to look for help, and I would explain things to them, and that is how I made many friends.

Oscar's mother refers to her son's abilities as "a computer-type of process." He grasps everything very fast. He does not have the patience to listen to the instructions being repeated for those children who do not understand. He needs to be always doing something; otherwise he gets bored and distracted and starts disturbing the class.

Oscar's fourth grade teacher played an important role in his greater academic achievement. Although Oscar describes her as a "solemn, cold, and extremely rigid teacher," the strong emphasis she put on reading, writing, and math helped Oscar achieve much higher academic performance. The teacher insisted on acceptable behavior, to the degree that, according to Oscar, the students "couldn't even move or talk." The students had to be always involved in some kind of activity, either completing an assignment, reading, writing, or simply thinking.

The results of such a rigorous, challenging, demanding, and busy climate were reflected in Oscar's citywide math and reading tests. The math percentile rank reported for the spring of 1995 was 91, and the percentile rank for the reading test was 79. Both scores were considerably higher than the previous year's. Oscar's family was thrilled with these results, and, without hesitation, his mother credited both the hardworking, rigid teacher and her bright, hardworking, dedicated son for such a wonderful and productive academic year.

Fifth Grade

Oscar started fifth grade with a full range of mixed feelings. On the one hand, he was very excited to think about the idea that in a year he would be going to middle school, meaning that he was no longer a child, he was growing and maturing, and that soon he would be able to do more "grown-up things." On the other, he and his family had to face the long, time-consuming task of finding the right junior high school that would meet Oscar's academic, social, and emotional needs. The idea of having to adjust to a new school environment made Oscar feel anxious and nervous. Fifth grade for Oscar was a good and productive year. The reported scores on the citywide tests were higher than the previous years.

Although fifth grade represented the last year for Oscar at the Lab School, it was not the last year for his mother. Oscar's younger brother is now attending the Lab School.

After all these years at the Lab School, Oscar acknowledges the great opportunities this school gave him to nurture and develop his talent potential. He recalls and celebrates his triumph over the troublesome transition and adjustment period, and the frustrating experience of being unable to communicate because of a lack of English proficiency.

> *Bueno, sí lo volvería a hacer definitivamente (repetir su vida académica en el Lab School). Esta es una escuela muy diferente, sobre todo si la comparo con P.S. 149. Lab School es grande, la forma en la que se enseñan aquí es muy buena, lo alimentan a uno y lo hacen pensar y trabajar todo el tiempo, todo lo entiendo perfectamente y me gusta. Hay mucha mezcla de niños y así uno conoce de todo, 149 es como muy cerrada y ademas como que nadie participa en nada, nunca se ven padres de familia participando en las actividades y ademas creo que nunca había nada para participar. En 149 como que toda la gente se escondían!*

> Well, definitely, I would do it again (repeat his school career at the Lab School). This is a very different school, above all if I compare it with P.S. 149. Lab School is big, the way they teach here is good, I understand perfectly well, and I like it. There is a large mix of kids, and you know many things. P.S. 149 is like very closed, and besides nobody participates in anything. You never see parents involved. At 149 it seemed that everybody was hiding!

The Search for the "Right Place"

Oscar's mother began to search for a middle school in the winter of 1995, when Oscar was in fifth grade. The process of finding the school that would meet Oscar's educational, social, emotional, and cultural needs was long, overwhelming, and daunting. The search began when Oscar's mother received a lengthy brochure containing information on the various middle schools in District #2 (the same District as the Lab School). The brochure described each school, including a brief introductory history of the school, the school's characteristics, its student population, its philosophy, and its admission process. Oscar's mother described her feelings of confusion and fear:

> *Yo me leí ese libro (Junior High schools en el Distrito #2), como esta escrito en inglés, español y en chino, el único que me faltó leer fue el chino! Yo me leí ese libro en inglés y en español y lo volví a leer y lo volví a leer! Me lo sabía casi de memoria, tan es así que me llené tanto de pánico y tenía tanto miedo de hacer una selección equivocada, que se me pasó la fecha para visitar las escuelas con los tours que ellos hacen. Eso fue lo único que no hice, hice todo lo demás. Yo estaba concentrada en leer las descripciones y características de las escuelas para poder hacer la decisión que cuando me dí cuenta, ya casi todas las fechas habían pasado.*

> I read the book (Junior High Schools in District #2). Since it's written in English, Spanish and Chinese, the only version I didn't read was the Chinese! I read that book in English and Spanish, and I read it again and again! I almost knew it by heart. I was so full of panic and was scared to make the wrong selection, that I forgot the date to visit the schools with the tours they conduct. I didn't do that, but I did the rest. I was concentrating on reading the descriptions and features of the schools to make a decision, but when I became aware, almost all the dates had gone by.

Oscar's mother was so desperate that she called one of the Directors of Project Synergy for help. Oscar's mother knew that not only would she get the help she needed from the staff of Project Synergy, but since they know the school system better than she does, they could perhaps advise her as to which school to look at first. The phone call proved to be very helpful, and Oscar's mother felt that "calm and confidence came back to her life." In a matter of days, Oscar's mother received another package containing information from different junior high schools in New York City, but this time it came from Project Synergy. The list was narrowed to those schools that, according to Project Synergy, could appropriately meet Oscar's academic needs. Even though the job looked easier, it was not, by any means, less stressful. Oscar's mother began her research.

> *Después de que recibí la lista (de Synergy) llamé a las escuelas para que me mandaran mas información y también el formulario de entrada (en la lista venían las fechas en las que teníamos que llamar para pedir los formularios). Para saber mas de algunas escuelas empecé a preguntar a maestras o gente conocida si sabían mas acerca de las escuelas. Estaban puestas todas mis fuerzas para encontrarle la escuela apropiada a Oscar, queria que él estuviera tan bien como en el Lab School.*

> As soon as I got Synergy's list I called the schools to request more information as well as the application form (the date in which we had to call the schools to request the application was in the list). I also started to ask people and teachers about the different schools. All my energy was devoted to find the right school for Oscar; I wanted him to do as well as he did in the Lab School.

One of the schools Oscar's family had their hearts and minds set on was the De La Salle Academy. Several factors contributed to this almost obsessive aspiration. De La Salle Academy is an independent middle school that serves gifted urban students, all of whom are members of ethnic minority groups, many of whom are economically disadvantaged. The De La Salle Academy promotes a strong sense of community among its students and encourages them to believe that they can be agents of change. In addition, Oscar and his family heard from the De La Salle Academy long before they had to be involved in middle school applications, because one of the components of the talent development aspect of Project Synergy is the mentorship program, in which the mentors are drawn from the De La Salle Academy to work with students identified by the project as potentially gifted. They always thought of this school as a good placement possibility, but they were positive once they visited it and talked to Brother Brian, the school's director.

The weeks that followed their visit to the school were as busy as they were stressful. Oscar and his mother spent long hours working and preparing for the admission exam. Everything needed to be perfect. His mother states, "he needed to be very strong, especially in reading, because in math he was doing very well." However, a couple of weeks after completing the long and stressful admission process for De La Salle Academy, the family's hopes faded away when they learned that Oscar was not accepted at the De La Salle Academy. Neither Oscar nor his mother understood why was he rejected; the only thing that was clear to them was the anger, frustration, and hopelessness they felt.

The picture got even darker when, at the same time Oscar's family got the rejection letter from the De La Salle Academy, they got a second rejection letter, but this time from St. Hilda's & St. Hugh's School, an independent coeducational Episcopal school. Again, they never knew why he was not accepted.

Although the whole family was experiencing a period of confusion, with more questions than answers, Oscar's mother did not give up. She was determined to find the right place for her bright, hardworking son. She visited a couple of schools, submitted the applications, worked and studied with Oscar for the admission tests, and finally Oscar was accepted by two special middle school programs: the Academic Special Progress Program at Wagner Middle School 167 and the Mott Hall School. The fact of having these two school options gave the family, finally, some relief and peace of mind. In addition, during the summer of our interviews, Oscar was participating in a summer program as part of the admission process for another school, the St. Aloysius School. Oscar was finally accepted into St. Aloysius School, and he stayed there through the end of eight grade. He received a partial scholarship, so he had to maintain a good academic record. Oscar was very happy there, and so was his mother, especially after a long and difficult period of uncertainty. Oscar was, apparently, in the right educational setting where, so far, his needs were being addressed.

Today Oscar attends Xavier High School, an independent Catholic High School in New York City. He completed ninth grade there and he is currently enrolled in the tenth grade. He receives partial financial assistance and he is maintaining a high grade point average.

Project Synergy: "A World I Wasn't Aware Of"

Looking at the mature, serious youngster who uses both English and Spanish in beautifully expressive ways and talks very enthusiastically about school, it becomes difficult to connect this person to a child who could have stayed in a low-achieving, detrimental school in Central Harlem.

The efforts of Project Synergy to find the unidentified ability among children who attended P.S. 149/207 and provide them with transitional services and tutoring; a family, especially the mother, who fought for a good education for her children, who constantly recognized her son's ability, and encouraged him to succeed and to work hard in school; and, the presence of certain personal characteristics, including high academic achievement, motivation, aspiration, dedication, ambition, and a sense of being special, all contributed to the current image we now have of Oscar. All factors were necessary for him to succeed.

Project Synergy made a strong impact on Oscar and his family. "My life, and certainly Oscar's, would have been very different"; that is how Oscar's mother started our conversation regarding Project Synergy. After moments of thought and reflection, Oscar's mother was able to articulate, throughout our interviews, what has she gained from the Project and the immense debt she has with the people involved in it.

Synergy me enseñó un mundo que no conocía. Desde que yo recibí la carta de que Oscar había sido seleccionado para el proyecto yo he hecho todo lo que Synergy me aconsejó. Participamos en todo, cualquier reunion que habia yo siempre estaba ahí, nunca me perdí nada.

Lo que me hizo participar en el proyecto fué que a mí siempre me ha interesado que mis hijos tuvieran una buena educación, que estuvieran bien guiados, en una buena escuela, con buenas experiencias. El venir a Synergy me hacía sentir bien, sabía que yo iba a encontrar algo bueno para mí y para Oscar. Nunca sentí que el venir aquí era perder el tiempo. Yo estaba muy contenta con Synergy porque sabía que era algo positivo para Oscar. Yo siempre pensaba que si esta gente de Synergy estaba preocupada por todos estos niños, pues tenían que estarle dando lo correcto en cuanto al programa de los Sábados y en el verano y también la recomendación del Lab School. Siempre tuve confianza, me dejé guiar por ellos porque realmente yo de escuelas y cosas especiales aquí en este país no conocía.

Que si yo volvería a participar en el proyecto? Sí, definitivamente sí. Fué una experiencia muy positiva. Oscar tuvo una excelente oportunidad, aprovechó muy bien el tiempo. Además me he dado cuenta que no todos los niños tienen el mismo nivel académico, hay niños que sobresalen y otros no tanto, como que si hay diferentes niveles. Oscar no esta nada mal. Yo siempre lo estoy empujando y trabajando con él para que este entre los mejores y ahora me doy cuenta de que él va muy bien, que ya está entre los mejores alumnos. El siente que capta y entiende las cosas muy rápido y yo lo veo.

Si yo pudiera darle un consejo a los padres con hijos con talento yo les diría que si se encuentran con la oportunidad de participar en un programa como Synergy, que la tomen. Yo sé que tuve mucha suerte pero yo aproveché la oportunidad que Synergy me ofrecía porque yo se que hay gente que también fué seleccionada y no participó. No hay que quedarse en la casa tranquila y esperar que las cosas le lleguen a uno, a veces hay que buscarlas y cuando se presentan hay que tomarlas.

Synergy showed me a world I wasn't aware of. Since I got the letter inviting Oscar to participate in the project, I've done everything Synergy had suggested to me. We always participated. I would attend all the meetings; I never missed one. What made it possible for me to participate in the Project was that I've always been interested in my children having a good education, with guidance, in a good school, with good experiences. Coming to Synergy made me feel great; I knew I always find something good for me and for Oscar. I never felt like I was wasting my time coming here. I was very happy with Synergy because I knew it was something positive for Oscar. I always thought that if the people from Synergy were concerned with all these children, then they would be giving them the right things regarding the Saturday program and the Summer program and also the recommendation of the Lab School. I always trusted them; I always let them guide me because actually, I didn't know anything about schools or special programs in this country.

Would I become involved in the Project again? Yes, definitely yes. It was a very positive experience. Oscar had an excellent opportunity, he made very good use of his time. Also, I realized that not all kids have the same academic level; there are outstanding children and there are others who aren't. So it seems that there are different levels. Oscar isn't doing so bad. I am always pushing him and working with him so he can be among the best, and now I realized that he is doing very well, he is among the best. He grasps and understands things very fast, and I've noticed that too.

If I could give parents of talented children any advice, I would tell them that if they ever have the opportunity to participate in a program like Synergy, to take it. I know I was very lucky, but I took advantage of the opportunity because I know of other people who were selected but did not participate. One should not stay at home and wait for things to come to us. Sometimes one has to look for them, and when they come one must grasp them.

Oscar himself recognizes the strong impact Synergy caused in his life. Right from the beginning, when he learned he was coming to Columbia University to a "special class," he was very happy. Everything was a new experience: visiting the university; the teachers of the project; his classmates; the materials they used in the classroom; the things they studied about; and especially, the great opportunity he had to be in a program where he could learn without being bored and realize he was able to process the information in such a fast way. Despite the fact that Oscar's lack of English proficiency initially caused him some difficulty understanding and communicating with everybody, he never really expressed a desire to have had full communication with the project in Spanish. It seems as if he knew that there was no alternative: he had to master the English language, and the sooner the better.

Now that Oscar is in high school he realizes how lucky he was to be part of the Project. "I was so young then that I couldn't see the advantages that this program would bring me in the long run, but I can see clearly now."

A Gift That Does Not Need a Special Program in Order to Be Nurtured

Oscar's talent potential was recognized early, and as such it was addressed early as well. However, Oscar has another strength and gift that was never directly addressed in an educational setting. He is fully bilingual. Oscar was in a bilingual program when he first entered school but this program functioned only as a transition into an all-English classroom. The bilingual program was not chosen because Oscar's family was looking for a program that could nurture his culture and language. He was placed there, according to Oscar's mother, because he did not speak English; there was no other alternative. Even though the fact that Oscar is bilingual was constantly reiterated throughout our interviews, Oscar's family never looked for, or intended to place him in, a bilingual program. According to Oscar's mother, a gifted bilingual school would have been a good option; however, Oscar's mother has never heard of that kind of school.

According to Oscar's mother, her children get the Spanish at home so they do not need a school for that purpose. The only thing that matters is to be in a good school and be prepared for the future.

Oscar himself feels very proud of being bilingual; he describes himself as "a very special person because I'm able to speak and understand things in two languages." In addition, with this "special gift" he is constantly able to assume altruistic roles as he helps people when they have trouble with either language. There is one single exception to Oscar's altruistic role: no help for his parents.

> *Mire que yo no hablo bien el inglés, lo entiendo y lo leo mejor de lo que lo hablo, pero en la casa nunca he dejado ser una carga para mis hijos en lo relacionado con el idioma. Si yo tengo que hablar en inglés busco la forma de hacerlo pero nunca les hago a mis hijos que ellos lo hagan por mí.*
>
> *Yo no quiero que ellos sientan que tienen la responsabilidad de hacerlo y además no quiero darles responsabilidades de adulto si luego quiero regañarlos como niños, entiende? En la casa mi esposo y yo enseñamos, si tenemos que ayudarlos primero entendemos y luego ayudamos.*

> Look, I am not very fluent in English. I understand it and read it better than I speak, because at home, I've never been a burden for my children regarding the language. I seek the way to do it, but I never make my children do it for me.
>
> I don't want them to feel responsible, and besides I don't want to give them adult's responsibilities if I want to scold them as children. Do you understand? At home, my husband and I teach. If we have to help them with their homework, we first understand it, and then help them.

Oscar's family is constantly sending him messages about what a wonderful thing it is being able to speak two languages. They are also always reinforcing cultural pride in the home.

> *La cuestión de la cultura también lo tienen en la casa (los hijos). Oscar tiene perfectamente claro que él es Hispano, se siente orgulloso de eso y todos lo saben y no lo digo solamente por el español, sino también por él mismo. Tiene todas las costumbres de mi país, esta muy bien identificado.*

Yo siempre he estado muy preocupada por mis hijos y gracias a Dios yo he tenido el tiempo de hacerlo y también darles la cuestión Hispana.

The culture issue, they (the children) also have it at home. Oscar is clear on the fact that he is Hispanic. He feels proud about it. And everyone knows it, and I'm not saying this because of the Spanish language, but also for him. He has my country's traditions, he's well identified.

I have always been very concerned for my children, and, thank God, I've always had the time to do it and also to teach them Hispanic issues.

Oscar is quite certain that being Hispanic is a good thing. His culture is important to him. He compares himself to other Hispanic children who deny their background, and he feels sorry for them. Both Oscar and his mother acknowledged the role the Lab School played in stressing the importance of the different cultures and languages the children brought to the school, and they felt relief that at St. Aloysius that same message was perpetuated since for Father Durkan, St. Aloysius principal, "a child should never lose his roots."

⚜

Chapter Seven

Gaby: "Confusion and Pain"

Background

Gaby is a tall, curious girl who is also happy and very playful. She will turn 14 in the summer of 2001. She is the youngest of two children in an intact family living in a low-income community on New York City's Upper West Side in a neighborhood described by her mother as mainly Hispanic. Gaby's sister is 4 years older than she is. The sister is shy and serious, and it is reported that, although they have different personalities, they have a positive relationship. Gaby's sister does very well academically and helps Gaby quite a lot with school matters, sometimes to the extreme of doing Gaby's homework.

Gaby was born in Santiago, in the Dominican Republic, as were her sister and her parents. The family moved to New York City in the winter of 1987, when Gaby was 6 months old. Since Gaby was 4 years old, she has suffered from asthma, a condition that, according to her mother, "appears to be worsening during the winter time and when she is under too much pressure."

Gaby's father was raised in Santiago. He used to work in the construction business in the Dominican Republic, and when they moved to the United States he had to find other jobs because of his lack of English proficiency. Although Gaby's father is interested in giving his daughters a good education, as well as helping them with homework and other school matters, his limited available time restricts his involvement in the schools.

Gaby's mother was also born and raised in Santiago. She comes from a family of professionals and hardworking people. She talks very proudly about her parents and siblings. One of her brothers is a cardiologist who used to live in Spain and who is now a well-known doctor in Santiago; the other one has a managerial position with a cigarette factory. Gaby's mother wants to become a teacher; in fact she was enrolled in an ESL program in order to improve her English skills. Two years ago she was taking college credits to become a teacher's aide.

Gaby is very attached to her grandmother, who spends periods of time in New York City, helping, teaching, and taking care of Gaby and her sister. According to Gaby's mother, her mother functions as such a positive "force" in Gaby's life that she considered sending Gaby to live with her in Santiago, an offer that Gaby would enthusiastically take.

Although Gaby's mother emphasized throughout our interviews the strong and close relationship she has with her family, as well as her desire to return to her homeland, she knows that, for now, it is not economically feasible to leave and that the United States represents the best option for her daughters' education. Gaby's mother has always demonstrated commitment and advocacy for Gaby and her sisters' education. She states that her desire to see her daughters in a good school, with a solid education and, eventually, with a good job is so strong that she is ready to make any sacrifice that is needed, even staying in New York City.

Gaby's Diverse School Experience

Gaby was a very alert, friendly, and happy child. Her mother recalls her curiosity from a very young age; she was always very verbal, perceptive, and able to carry on conversations with adults in a manner beyond that expected of a child her age.

Gaby has great drawing ability; in fact, she states that not only is drawing the thing she likes to do best, but also she admits doing it very well. Since she was a little girl, her drawings have been very representational, full of detail and color.

Gaby's school career started when she was three years old, and her mother registered her part time in the local Head Start program so *"ella aprendiera a ir a la escuela y a quedarse"* (she could learn to go to school and stay there). The Head Start experience was a very positive one, and Gaby spent two happy and productive years there. When it was time for Gaby to go to kindergarten, a group of people came to the Head Start school and talked to the parents about the program at the Family School, located in Central Harlem, New York City. According to Gaby's mother, this is a school that has a good program, and the children learn a lot. It also has strong parental involvement and special English programs for non-English speaking parents. However, according to Gaby's mother, transportation issues and the fact that the English program conflicted with Gaby's mother's schedule resulted in its being not such a good option for them. Gaby attended the Family School for only one week.

When Gaby's mother realized that she no longer had a school for Gaby, she went to Public School 192 for help. P.S. 192 is an elementary school in Community School District 6, which was their district when they used to live near that school. Gaby's sister was attending that school, so her mother decided to send Gaby there, not only because she wanted to place them in the same school, but also because she knew the director, the teachers, and she was convinced that it was a good school because of M's (Gaby's sister) great academic performance. However, Gaby's mother was totally unprepared for the response she got from the school. Gaby could not attend that school because that was no longer her district. Her mother could not understand the lack of flexibility in the school's argument. She found it difficult to accept the argument that by moving a couple of blocks north of Manhattan, the school district changes. Also, if it is stated as a fact that people from out of the district could not attend P.S. 192, how come she knew children who were registered at P.S. 192 and lived in the Bronx. And finally, Gaby's mother took it for granted that P.S. 192 would accept Gaby since her sister was attending the school since kindergarten, and it makes sense to have siblings registered in the same school. What frustrated and annoyed her the most, however, was the powerlessness of the school's director and her lack of understanding toward Gaby's circumstances, especially since Gaby's mother was honest with the school regarding her new location.

Gaby's mother knew she could have gotten her into the school with a distorted story; however, her moral values prevented her from doing it.

Knowing that there was no other alternative, Gaby's mother registered her at their local public school. However, because they missed the registration period, their neighborhood school could not take her, so, as in Oscar's case, Gaby was transferred to P.S. 149/207 in Central Harlem, New York City. Gaby was placed in the kindergarten bilingual program. P.S. 149/207 is where I met Gaby and her mother for the first time, when I was a consultant teacher for Project Synergy.

During our interviews neither Gaby nor her mother talked much about P.S. 149/207. Neither complained about the school, and it seems that they both have spent happy times there. Gaby made some friends and she was doing fine academically. Gaby did not have to suffer the consequences of lacking English proficiency because, although the kindergarten program was labeled as "bilingual," most of the time the children spoke Spanish.

Gaby's mother's involvement with the school was very limited; basically she just talked to the teacher when she needed to. She did not participate in school activities because she did not feel that she belonged there; after all, she did not select that school as her first option.

By the end of the kindergarten year, Gaby's teacher talked to her mother about Project Synergy, explaining to her that Gaby was selected to participate in this special project funded by the federal government to find children with high academic promise and provide special services for them. Given that Gaby's teacher had previous experience with Project Synergy because Oscar was in her classroom, she eagerly encouraged Gaby's mother to participate, stressing the great opportunity for Gaby. Soon after this conversation I visited Gaby's mother at her home in order to explain to her all the details and specifics about the program. Without hesitation she agreed to participate in the Project, beginning in the summer of 1993.

By the end of kindergarten Gaby's mother requested that Gaby be transferred back to her neighborhood school (P.S. 153) because going to P.S. 149/207 was somewhat difficult. Having this request granted, Gaby was placed in an all-English classroom for first grade at P.S. 153, and, apparently, things went well; neither Gaby nor her mother talked much about that first grade experience.

The communication between Project Synergy and Gaby's family continued during Gaby's first grade year. She not only attended Project Synergy's Saturday Enrichment and Summer Programs, but her mother was able to explore several educational options under Synergy's suggestion and guidance. One such was Patrick Henry, a special program designed exclusively for children identified as gifted. This special program, which is housed in Public School 171, has its own administration, faculty, admission requirements, and curriculum. Although Gaby's parents liked the program and the school, they decided not to pursue the admission process because they learned that the school did not provide bus service. In addition, Gaby's sister was not going to be able to attend the same school, and this time they were very determined to register both of them in the same school. According to Gaby's mother, the people from Patrick Henry recommended Central Park East (CPE) School, as a school that might meet their family needs.

Even though Gaby's parents visited the school and talked to the principal, they were never fully informed about the progressive philosophy of CPE. Gaby's parents liked the school, they completed the application form and in a matter of weeks both Gaby and her sister were registered at CPE II (the elementary school), in second and sixth grade respectively.

Although this school represented an opportunity for Gaby to be in an educationally competitive program, it also represented the beginning of a painful and confusing period. Gaby only attended the CPE School for second and third grade.

Confusion and Pain

The CPE School is a public school located in Community School District 4 in New York City. The school enrolls students from Pre-K through 12 grade, divided into two separate buildings, one for the elementary school, which is actually called CPE II, and the other for the Secondary School, located a couple of blocks away. CPE, as a brochure describes them, "is a school that gives both teachers and students high amounts of personal freedom for development." CPE II is considered to be a small elementary school, since it has a maximum enrollment of 173 students, with a maximum of 20 students per class. Some classes are multiage grouped; others are not. CPE II's approach to education is child-centered and progressive. According to one of the teachers working at the school, "children have a voice in how their classroom operates; children and teachers work together to plan part of the curriculum and part of the activities; no textbooks or workbooks are part of the daily activities." All classrooms are interactive and hands-on. Emphasis is placed on real-world problem solving, building life-long literacies and a love of language and the arts. Literature plays a big part in the school curriculum. CPE II has Spanish language, science, physical education and music for all children. It also has resource rooms for those children in need of special attention. Application to the school is open to all students in New York City, regardless of their Community School District.

Coming from two years' experience with Project Synergy's Summer and Saturday Enrichment Programs, and her mother's evaluation that she had a smart little girl who would be attending a good school, Gaby entered second grade in a first-second bridge classroom with a positive and happy attitude. Although the second grade year was, by no means, an easy one, Gaby was able to adapt to the new environment, and, in fact, she repeatedly mentioned during our interviews how happy she was and how much she loved that school. However, this year marked the beginning of severe academic difficulties that, unfortunately, the family was not aware of until the end of third grade, when they decided to pull Gaby out of the school and place her in their more traditional neighborhood public school. Gaby's mother explained:

> Gaby está muy contenta en la escuela. Pero yo no estoy contenta. A mí no me gusta el sistema de la clase. En sí yo no sé cómo funciona muy bien. Nunca trajo tarea y lo poco que le daban era para que la regrese en tres semanas y además era muy simple, la terminaba en unos minutos. Un niño no puede aprender así, todos los días tiene que repasar y estudiar algo! También para las vacaciones no le dieron nada para trabajar. Imagínate tantas semanas y la muchacha sin hacer nada de la escuela. Yo no veía que Gaby tenía problemas, solamente me daba cuenta que las niñas del edificio, que iban a otra escuela, siempre estaban trabajando, les daban tarea todos los días y estudiaban bien. Lo único que le vi traer a Gaby fueron varios proyectos que

hizo, eran de mucha manualidad e investigación y eso a ella le en-cantа.

Gaby is very happy at school. But I'm not happy. I don't like the classroom system. I actually don't know how it works so well. She never had homework, and the little she had had to be handed back in three weeks, and it was very simple; she completed it in a few minutes. A child cannot learn this way; they have to study every day! Also, they didn't give her anything to work on during the holidays. Just imagine, so many weeks and the girl doesn't do any schoolwork. I didn't realize that Gaby had problems, I only noticed that the girls in the building, who attend a different school, they were always working, they got homework every day, and they studied well. The only thing that I saw Gaby working on was a couple of projects. She had to do research and art and she loves that.

Gaby's mother talked to the teacher on several occasions to request more homework for her, but Gaby's mother was still not very pleased with the school. She even visited the classroom a couple of times to see an actual school day, but that did not help either. It took Gaby's parents a while to realize and understand that the school has a different philosophy and academic style. According to Gaby's mother's comments, her view of a good education is related to a more traditional view of education: one with no mixed-age groups; where the students get daily homework, work on specific problems and topics in the classroom, and more emphasis is placed on academic areas such as reading, writing, and math.

It is interesting to point out that Gaby's parents' lack of understanding of and belief in CPE's progressive education as a good education exemplifies Delpit's (1995) observation that "beliefs about what constitutes good teaching vary across different cultural communities" (p. 139). Delpit goes on to explain that the relationship among the teacher, the student, and the content can be viewed in different ways by different communities. Gaby's parents interpret the role of education through their own cultural lens and experience, and it is difficult for them to understand that other approaches and philosophies of education do exist.

Attributing Gaby's lack of academic progress to the peculiar and nontraditional classroom system, Gaby's parents decided to keep her in that school for another year and to give her a chance to get used to that educational style, hoping that things would get better.

Although the parents felt initially that they had made a good decision, it became obvious very quickly that Gaby was not making a good academic progress in her second year in that school. Gaby was placed in a third-fourth-bridge classroom, with a new teacher and some new classmates. However, as the year went by, not only did her academic performance not improve, but also now she was identified as a child with severe academic difficulties. As could be expected, these academic difficulties had emotional consequences. Gaby's teacher explained:

> I always found that Gaby, although she is a very, very sweet girl, got very frustrated if I asked her to do something again or to do it a little more carefully.
> Although her reading skills were not at grade level, she did things very quickly, sometimes so quickly that she missed important things.
> Things weren't done right or well. And she would get very, very upset.

Her classroom teacher felt that extra attention would help Gaby overcome some of her difficulties, so she recommended her for resource room. Gaby was pulled out from the classroom for special and remedial instruction in basic skills once a day. However, this special instruction did not prove to be very successful. Gaby's academic performance did not improve.

Gaby's mother was very concerned and distressed. She was painfully aware that Gaby's poor academic performance was due to a lack of reading and writing ability.

> *Gaby no va bien en cuanto a lectura y escritura, no está mejorando para nada. Ella no sabe lo suficiente, digamos que no está al nivel que debería estar.*

> Gaby is not doing well in reading and writing; she's not improving at all. She doesn't know enough; in other words, she's not at the level she's supposed to be on.

It was not until this time that Gaby's mother took an active advocacy role and went out searching for help. She sought advice from M's (Gaby's sister) second grade teacher at P.S. 192 because, according to Gaby's mother, that teacher was "the best," and M's academic achievement improved quite a lot when she was with that teacher.

> *Yo hablé con la maestra y le dije cómo Gaby estaba y los problemas que tenía y ella me dijo que la pasaramos a esa escuela que ahí sí iba a aprender. Me recuerdo muy bien como dijo la maestra "ella aquí va a aprender, traiganla para acá." También ella nos dió todos los libros de tercer grado porque a Gaby no le habían dado nada y también todos, todos los folletos que habían dado durante el año para que practique y lo hizo. Son folletos, como hojas solas, por ejemplo, donde hay dibujos que tienen que recortar y pegarlo junto al nombre de las cosas.*

I spoke to the teacher and told her about Gaby's situation and the problems she had and she told us to enroll her in that school, because there she was going to learn. I recalled how the teacher said "here she is going to learn, bring her here." Also, she gave us all the third grade books, because Gaby had not received anything and also all, all the brochures they had given during the year so she can practice, and she did it. They are brochures, like sheets of paper, for instance with drawings; they have to cut and paste them near the name of the things.

Even though Gaby's mother had to find what she believed was in Gaby's best interest—which in this case was providing, and even transferring her to, a more traditional type of education with plenty of homework, textbooks, and worksheets—Gaby was by no means happy about that. She even became adversarial and opposed to working on the worksheets and textbooks. Throughout our interviews, Gaby indignantly reacted to her mother's plan. In some cases she tried to cover her mouth to prevent her from criticizing the school, and in others she was sure to communicate her disagreement over being transferred to their local public school.

> *GABY: A mí me encanta mi escuela, you know that we play kickball. But the thing that I like the best is music, I love music. I also like art and gym. Yo ya le dije a Mami mil veces que a mí no me gusta ninguna otra escuela, yo no me quiero ir a ninguna otra escuela! Las hojas que Mami trajo de la otra escuela no me gustan, a mí me gusta mi escuela.*

GABY: I love my school, you know that we play kickball. But the thing that I like the best is music; I love music. I also like art and gym. I told Mami like a thousand times that I don't like any other school; I don't want to go to any other school! I don't like the sheets that Mami brought from the other school; I like my school.

INVESTIGADORA: Gaby cuéntame qué te gusta de la escuela? Todo me gusta, yo me quiero quedar ahí. A mi no me gusta la escuela de aquí cerca. No me gusta porque ahí no se llevan bien (los chicos y las maestras), tratan a los chicos mal y yo he oído que les jalan los oidos a los que no estudian bien! Además les gritan a los muchachos, no los tratan bien. Yo sé que Mami me quiere cambiar a otra escuela y yo no quiero. Yo sé que esa escuela (escuela del vecindario) no es buena, I know that. Yo nunca voy a estar felíz en otra escuela.

RESEARCHER: Gaby tell me what do you like about school? Everything, I want to stay there. I don't like the school nearby. I don't like it because they don't get along (teachers and students); they mistreat the children, I heard that they pull the ears of those who are not good students! Besides, they yell at the kids; they are not well treated. I know that Mami wants to transfer me to another school, and I don't want to. I know it is not a good school (local public school), I know that. I'm never going to be happy in any other school.

It is interesting to note that even though Gaby knew about her mother's plans to transfer her to P.S. 153, their local public school, and that she was in the resource room because of her need for special attention, she never outwardly expressed frustration or anger or that she was being teased by her classmates because of her disability. She never compared herself, at least during our interviews, with the other children. It seems as if, in the classroom, Gaby tried to compensate for her academic difficulties by utilizing her superior social skills, keeping her self-esteem, at least socially speaking, at a high level. She was very popular, had plenty of friends, and was well liked by the other students.

However, Gaby's academic struggles could not be solved or ignored by being the "popular kid." At one point, Gaby's teacher thought that Gaby's lack of English proficiency could be the cause of her academic difficulties. So she requested a Spanish-speaking teacher's aide to spend time in her classroom to assist her.

Knowing that Gaby's problem might be related to a language barrier, her teacher tried to accommodate Gaby's needs by giving her special attention and consideration. However, she realized that Gaby's problems went beyond the language barrier.

> I kept on thinking about her (Gaby), and when I see her working in the class on math problems or reading assignments, I think that maybe it is not just a language issue, maybe it is in the processing of information.

Near the end of the third grade year, Gaby took the citywide reading and math tests. It was these tests, together with the resource room teacher's evaluation, that finally confirmed Gaby's learning disability. The percentile rank for the reading test was 2, and for the math it was 14, both dramatically below the state standard. The resource room teacher thought that Gaby would be better served in a special education class as opposed to a resource room. The classroom teacher then recommended that a thorough psychoeducational evaluation be done.

At first, Gaby's father rejected this idea, but Gaby's mother insisted on allowing the school to do the testing so they "could prove that Gaby is a normal child, that she doesn't have psychological problems and the school is the one that is wrong, or let's say that this system didn't work for G."

The educational evaluation concluded that Gaby had a learning disability, causing academic delays in reading, writing and math. It was suggested that Gaby's academic needs could be better met in a "Supplemental Instructional Services I," a special education class where she would get the special attention she needed. Gaby's parents were astonished, angry, and very confused. They would never allow their daughter to be placed in a special education class. They believed that the school's different academic philosophy was the cause of Gaby's problems. According to them:

> *La escuela tiene que ver de que Gaby no aprendió. Yo digo que si Gaby se hubiera quedado en una escuela tadicional, ella hubiera aprendido también, ella supiera igual que M (la hermana de Gaby).*

> The school has something to do with the fact that Gaby didn't learn. I say that had Gaby stayed in a traditional school, she would have also learned, she would know the same as M (Gaby's sister).

Now, more than ever, Gaby's parents decided it was time to find a different educational setting for their daughter, and the only option they were familiar with and trusted was their local public school. Gaby's parents never sought a second opinion regarding the diagnosis, nor did they search for other options or opportunities. Against Gaby's will, they concluded that she was going to attend their local public school and was going to need to repeat third grade.

Even though Gaby's classroom teacher supported the parents' decision of holding her over because this "would in fact be beneficial for her," she obviously disagreed with the decision to pull her out of the school. As she stressed:

> It is really sad to hear that she is leaving us. And there are those feelings in me, too, that I didn't do a good job with her because she is not where she should be. She really is behind.
>
> People who evaluated Gaby said that, when the mother moves her to a different school, she will find out it wasn't the school. Gaby has the problem, and she needs help.

Gaby's classroom teacher tried to talk to the mother, but she did not listen or understand the problem. The only thing Gaby's mother could understand was her pain and confusion. Evidently, Gaby's family did not accept the fact that she had a learning disability, or, at best, they thought her learning difficulties were bothersome but not terribly significant. This belief was supported by three assertions. First, Gaby's parents attributed their daughter's lack of academic progress and poor academic performance to CPE's progressive educational system. Second, Project Synergy's message was that Gaby is a bright child. And third, Gaby's mother acknowledged and believed that:

> *Yo he hecho muchos errores con Gaby en cuanto a escuelas. Ella ha estado en un mundo entero de escuelas, eso es lo que a ella la ha perjudicado mas, que no ha estado en la misma escuela todo el tiempo, no ha estado estable.*
>
> I've made many mistakes with Gaby as far as schools are concerned. She has been in so many schools, that is what has harmed her more, that she has not attended the same school all the time, she has not been stable.

Gaby's parents were determined to help her, as they have always done. They were full of hope that P.S. 153 would indeed be the solution to Gaby's disability and that, eventually, she would be a better student.

When Gaby began attending her local public school in a regular third grade, her mother felt they had made the right decision. According to Gaby's mother she made gradual progress in acquiring academic skills.

It is perplexing and uncertain if indeed P.S. 153 was the right place and had the right teacher to assist Gaby in meeting her needs. While Gaby was attending third grade at P.S. 153 the family contemplated the possibility of moving back to their homeland. There is no information regarding the family's move, whether it was provisional or permanent. In addition, there is no data available on Gaby's academic life after P.S. 153. It was not possible to contact the family again. The last reported information was obtained while Gaby was in third grade at P.S. 153. The mother said that Gaby "seems to be happy in her new school and with her new friends." Most likely Gaby's family continues to be her strong advocates, helping her, supporting her, focussing on her verbal and social strengths, and especially sending her messages about what a wonderful, friendly, and joyful person she is.

Project Synergy: "A Positive but Short Experience"

Gaby was identified as potentially gifted by Project Synergy when she was in kindergarten at P.S. 149/207. She became part of the third cohort of the project. Given that Gaby was enrolled in the bilingual kindergarten classroom, and the predominant language used in that classroom was Spanish, the entire identification process was done in Spanish, so none of the students in that classroom would be penalized because of a lack of English proficiency. She was identified as a highly verbal and social child who also had great drawing ability. Her drawings were very representational, full of color and detail.

Gaby was invited to participate in the five-week summer program in the summers following her kindergarten and first grade years and on weekends during those academic years. These two years were the only experience she had with the project. Gaby's mother was invited to participate in workshop for parents, which were held concurrently with the transitional services classes. Both Gaby and her mother actively and consistently participated in the transitional services.

Even though Gaby's mother reported that participating in the project was a "positive and worthwhile experience" and that, in general, she was happy while in the project, she also confessed her dissatisfaction and confusion regarding Gaby's academic difficulties as they related to the project. Apparently, an evaluation of her academic progress never occurred during her involvement with Project Synergy.

Gaby's mother would have liked to have more communication with the people from Project Synergy, and also she would have liked them to advise her regarding Gaby's reading and writing difficulties. However, Gaby's mother never sought guidance, either from the people of Project Synergy or from anybody else, until Gaby was in third grade, when she talked to a teacher at P.S. 192. More communication and involvement were needed regarding Gaby's school adjustment, as well as an assessment or appraisal of her academic progress.

Gaby reported herself to be very happy when she was participating in the Project's transitional services. She never reported, during our interviews, having had any difficulty with reading or writing, understanding and communicating in English, or any other sort of problem while in the project.

Overall, Gaby's mother thought that, despite the fact that their participation in the project was a very short one, it was a positive one indeed, and that they, certainly, would become involved in the project again.

Pride and Respect for Being Hispanic

Gaby's family came to the United States hoping to attain a better and more stable economic life, and that is exactly what has kept them in this country for more than 15 years. They knew that they would be coming into a country that, in spite of the many rich possibilities it might offer, was frightening and new, with a different language and culture. Over the course of the years, both the mother and the father had spent time learning English, so that this "necessity" would not interfere with their dreams.

Gaby's parents are very precise as to what message they want their daughters to obtain regarding their cultural and linguistic background. They are Hispanics and, as such, they not only need to speak Spanish, but they also need to be familiar with their background, live like Hispanics, and feel proud of who they are. The most important value, according to Gaby's mother, is for the girls to learn to respect themselves and others. As the mother declared:

> *Es muy importante que mis hijas hablen su idioma (el español). Nunca deben de olvidarse de su idioma. Ellas se tiene que sentir orgullosas de lo que son, aunque estén en el país que estén y aprendan cualquier otro idioma, ellas tienen que conservar sus raíces y se tienen que acordar de dónde vienen. El respeto a sí mismas y el comprender a las demás personas es lo más importante que tienen que aprender.Yo me he comprado algunos libros en español para poder explicarles mejor todo lo de nuestro país y que ellas sepan todo. También tratamos de ir o mandarlas a la República Dominicana y estén ahí y las saquen y conozcan. También lo único que comemos en la casa es dominicano, si no hay arroz todos los días, porque el arroz es de lo más típico y la base en nuestra comida, mis hijas dicen que les falta a la comida.*

It is very important that my daughters speak in their own language (Spanish). You must never forget your language. They must feel proud of who they are. Even if they live in the country and learn any language, they must always preserve their roots and must always remember where they come from. Self-respect and understanding other people is the most important thing they need to learn. I bought some books in Spanish to be able to better explain all about our country and read with them so they can know. We also try to go or send them to the Dominican Republic and be there and take them out and become familiar with it. Besides, at home we only eat Dominican food. If there is not rice every day, because rice is our most typical and basic food, they say something is missing.

Gaby's mother admitted she would have loved to have Gaby attend a bilingual elementary school. She even expressed regret over their decision to enroll Gaby in an all-English program. Gaby's mother is in favor of bilingual education, not only because she believes it is what is best for every child with Hispanic back-ground, but also because M (Gaby's sister) attended a bilingual program from kindergarten through first grade with, according to Gaby's mother, outstanding academic performance.

However, Gaby's mother never really pursued her desire to see Gaby enrolled in a bilingual program. She was not aware of any bilingual program that would nurture their Hispanic culture and language, rather than just a bilingual program that serves as a transition to an all-English program. It would have been a good option back then, but currently she does not think that a bilingual program would be the best option for Gaby.

> *Bueno, la verdad es que ahora yo estoy muy confundida. Yo no creo que ahora un programa bilingüe la beneficiaría mucho por lo que ella no sabe bien leer ni escribir en inglés, mucho menos en español. Creo que la atrasaría más.*

> Well, the truth is that I am very confused. I don't think that a bilingual program would benefit her a lot because she does not know how to read and write in English, much less in Spanish. I think that would delay her.

Gaby herself likes to use both Spanish and English to commu-nicate with her family and friends. She looks forward every sum-mer to going to the Dominican Republic and spending time there with her extended family, and "get all the Spanish and Dominican food she wants." She loves, and feels proud of, being Hispanic and everything related to being Hispanic.

Chapter Eight

Tina: "She Needs a Special School..."

Background

Tina is an energetic, outgoing, and very social girl who will turn 11 in the winter of 2000. She lives with her mother, and periodically her grandmother spends periods of time with them. Tina has limited contact with and little knowledge of her father. Tina was born in New York City.

Tina's mother is a smart, active and ambitious woman who was born and raised, by her mother solely, in New York City. Both of her parents were born in the Dominican Republic and came to the United States as young adults. Although Tina's mother understands and speaks Spanish fluently, she feels more comfortable communicating in English; therefore, our interviews were carried on mostly in English. Tina's mother comes from a family of musicians and singers. Both her grandfather and father were musicians, and her mother was a singer. Tina's mother recalls that in spite of always having "a passion, desire, and ability to learn," she had a difficult childhood in terms of her academic experience and educational opportunities. As the next excerpt shows, when Tina's mother was in elementary school, she not only got negative attention for being smart, but her teachers did not know what to do with her:

> When I was young I was labeled as the problem child that got moved from classroom to classroom because they didn't know what to do with me. I was never labeled as gifted; however I did very well in school. There was really no grade skipping in the higher elementary school grades, so I was shifted from classroom to classroom without

> anyone searching for a solution to my problem. I remember being
> bored easily; nothing was like...challenging. Though I had the ability
> to learn, there was no proper program in place to help me excel.

It was not until junior high school that Tina's mother's school experience changed, when she was labeled "smart" and was registered in a Catholic school for "academically advanced students."

Tina's mother got a bachelor's degree in music therapy at the New School for Social Research, in New York City. She plans to continue with a master's degree within the same field.

Tina's mother takes the primary responsibility for Tina's education. She acknowledges her daughter's talent and abilities, and since Tina was a little girl she has been very involved in and devoted to getting her the best educational options possible.

I met Tina and her mother for the first time when I was working as a consultant teacher for Project Synergy Preschool, a project that began operation in 1993, as an outgrowth of Project Synergy. This new project extended Project Synergy's goals of identifying and educating potentially gifted students from economically disadvantaged backgrounds and culturally different groups to a preschool population (in day care centers) and provided services to the children, their families, and their teachers. Tina was part of a first cohort of 14 children identified as potentially gifted.

Signs of Precocity and Early School Exposure

Tina's mother was aware of her daughter's potential and felt from very early on that she was "very, very smart. She has a great and impressive memory, she could remember things that happened days and even weeks before, she would remember everything."

Tina has always been very verbal, outgoing, and especially perceptive. She was able to carry on conversations in a manner beyond that expected of a child her age. Tina's mother confesses that her daughter's superb communication ability and understanding of complex topics allows her to be "open" with her. As she stated:

I know that if I need to emphasize and talk to Tina on the importance of using her talent and potential in a positive and productive
way, she will understand me. Also, I'm always trying to tell her that
she is smart, but that doesn't mean that she has to forget the rules.
She has to respect people. Also, I always encourage her to talk about
her feelings and ideas, you know, if there is something wrong we talk
about it.

Tina has shown great drawing ability since she was a little
girl. Her mother recalls their apartment walls being full of "color-
ful murals. She used to draw everywhere and on everything." Now
that she is older, it is still possible to find magnificent samples of
her drawings on her books, notebooks, or just on pieces of paper.
Her drawings are becoming more sophisticated, rich in detail and
color.

Tina likes to read and write. When she was a little girl, she
used to like to be read to, now she likes to read by herself or read
to her mother or grandmother.

Tina has always been a social child. Ever since she was a little
girl she enjoyed the company of other children, and although
sometimes she had to overcome the consequences of being a single
child by learning to share toys and adult attention, she managed
to enjoyed herself and have fun with other children.

Tina's first school experience began when she was almost
three years old and her mother registered her at Grant Day Care
Center, a community-based day care center located in New York
City's Upper West Side. The center has a maximum enrollment of
350 children, including preschool and school age children, ages
from 2.9 to 12 years old. Tina started at the center being Spanish-
language dominant; however, her limited English proficiency did
not interfere with her adjustment at the center. She immediately
acquired the English and became fully bilingual.

Tina's first year at the center was favorable in terms of her
development and growth. Her language and motor ability rapidly
developed, and her social skills increased even more. She became
more English-language dominant but still was able to understand
and speak in Spanish. She enjoyed playing with pretend and
imaginative materials. And she loved interacting with her classmates; she was well liked by the other children.

Before Project Synergy Preschool began with the identification process the director of the center had informed all the preschool parents about the project's goals and procedures, and that was the first time Tina's mother heard about Project Synergy Preschool. Tina was identified as a child with exceptional potential.

Tina's exceptional potential suggested that she could benefit from an enriched classroom experience, so she was invited to participate in Project Synergy Preschool's five-week Summer Enrichment Program that was held during the summer of 1994.

By the end of the academic school year, Tina was moved to one of the kindergarten classrooms, instead of group 3, the last preschool classroom of the center. Both the teachers and the director thought that she was not only emotionally and academically ready for the challenges of kindergarten, but she was old enough to be placed in that classroom. Tina was going to turn 5 by the end of the year.

The Challenge of Coordinating
a Variety of Educational Settings

The new academic year that Tina was about to start was not only fundamental to her recently started educational career, but it also represented a year of new, enriched, and demanding academic experiences. Several events and people were instrumental in bringing about development and progress in Tina's talent potential and positive attitude toward school during this year. First of all, Tina was enrolled in a brand new kindergarten classroom at Grant Day Care Center, which she was attending in the morning. Second, Tina was sponsored at the Hollingworth Preschool, a private preschool for gifted children at Teachers College, during the 1994–1995 academic year, where she joined the afternoon session. Finally, Tina was attending the Saturday Enrichment Program as part of Project Synergy Preschool's transitional services during the weekend. So, practically speaking, Tina's day began at her kindergarten classroom at Grant Day Care Center, then, at midday, she had to be escorted from the center to the Hollingworth Preschool so she could join the afternoon class, and finally, she had to be picked up by her mother or grandmother from the preschool. Plus, she had to attend the special program on she had to attend the special program on Saturdays. These new educational arrangements, clearly, required the cooperation and collaboration of the people from Project Synergy Preschool, Grant Day Care Center, the Hollingworth Preschool, and, indisputably, from Tina's family.

The Hollingworth Preschool is an outgrowth of the Leta Hollingworth Center founded in 1981 at Teachers College, Columbia University, in New York City. The Hollingworth Preschool program was designed to provide an optimal early childhood program for young children whose atypical cognitive abilities require a differentiated educational setting (Wright & Coulianos, 1991). The mission of the Hollingworth Preschool, according to the director, is to provide an optimal educational match between the needs of the bright, creative, and curious children it serves, and a developmentally appropriate and responsive early childhood environment.

Although Tina's enrollment in the Hollingworth Preschool was viewed as a much needed and positive move, it was not completely free of conflicts and challenges. This was due not only to scheduling arrangements and logistics involved but also, and mainly, to significant differences between the two settings. The Grant Day Care Center and the Hollingworth Preschool differ in philosophical foundation, admission process, curriculum, faculty, parent body, facilities, and size. In terms of Tina's actual day, it represented a transition from a formal, traditionally structured academic environment with 25 classmates and two teachers, to a classroom with 15 classmates, two teachers and a child-responsive curriculum within a verbally rich environment that fosters curiosity, thinking, and imagination.

According to Tina's mother, "it took Tina a while to get adjusted to this new schedule, but after some time she got kind of used to going back and forth."

Tina had a very busy but productive year; as her mother pointed out "she did too many things during the week." She continued describing what she called "a roller coaster ride":

> It was non-stop; Tina was always doing something! I was always amazed at the things she would tell me she was learning. She knows more about astronomy, insects, dinosaurs, and anatomy than I ever

did at her age. She was allowed to explore learning on her own. She was also allowed to be part of the decision making. She was a happy kid.

It is worth emphasizing that Tina's good adjustment and pleasant experience at all three educational settings was the result of the effort of the teachers at Grant Center which went beyond mere cooperation to enthusiastic support; the care and dedication of the people from Hollingworth Preschool; the assurance and determination of the staff of Project Synergy Preschool to give Tina the opportunity to be in the appropriate educational setting as well as to provide her with enriched educational experiences; the continuous involvement and advocacy of Tina's mother; and, finally, Tina's special personal characteristics, including her ability and flexibility to adapt to new and different environments, her sophisticated social skills, and high academic aptitude and talent potential.

Project Synergy Preschool: "A Very Special Experience Both for T and Me"

Tina was identified as potentially gifted when she was four and one-half years old, and was attending Grant Day Care Center. Even though the identification activities could have been conducted in Spanish, the whole process was done with Tina in English, given her acceptable level of English proficiency. She was identified as a child with ample and sophisticated social skills as well as academic potential; her memory and problem solving skills were quite remarkable.

Tina was invited to participate in the five-week summer program following her identification, in the fall and spring weekend sessions during the 1994–1995 academic year. Tina was sponsored at the Hollingworth Science Enrichment Camp, a program that, according to the camp's brochure, "provides students with an introduction to and appreciation of life sciences, physical sciences, biological sciences, and environmental sciences in their everyday lives." The curriculum used is developmentally appropriate and it emphasizes the "doing" of science.

Tina actively and consistently participated in the several enrichment programs she encountered. In brief, Tina's mother pointed out that "the whole experience was very special both for Tina and me." As she pointed out:

> At first I was kind of worried because too many things happened at the same time: the Day Care, Synergy, and Hollingworth. But every program was perfectly organized. You did a wonderful job communicating with me about all three programs, and also the Day Care always gave me lots of information about what was going on there. I didn't feel a lack of information or communication. For Tina it was…wooohh…I can learn in different places. I remember how much she loved the Saturday Program. She was extremely happy; she waited for it all week. I could see that she, well you, did a lot with all these kids. The project helped me to see what kind of a school I would like for her because I wanted something similar to what you gave her. It is extremely difficult to find a good program. I screened lots of programs for her. I thought about a private school, but then I thought I could not afford it. Then mmm…I realized that a public school was the perfect choice. I never thought about the next school so closely until I started talking to you guys and I came to the kindergarten orientation meeting. It was a great help and guidance. We had a great experience; we loved it. Everything that we came across with was wonderful; everything that needed to be done was done. We were really very happy. The only thing was the time period; it was too short. Just when you start, it was already over. I would have loved a much longer program, like a school-type thing.

Project Synergy Preschool had, indeed, a strong impact on Tina and her family. As her mother said, "you really had an impact on these kids and us, and we all appreciate it a lot."

By the time their involvement with Project Synergy Preschool ended, Hollingworth Preschool's and Grant Day Care Center's academic year also came to term. Tina was ready to move to a first grade classroom.

"T Needs a Special School for Gifted Children"

Tina's mother was convinced that her daughter needed to continue her education in a school environment as special, challenging and rich as the previous ones. As she stated in her own words:

> Tina has to attend a school for gifted children. A school that really gives these kids something different, because you know that some schools just give special names to their programs, but they really don't do anything special with those kids. Sometimes it's just the name.

It is interesting to point out that even though Tina's mother had direct and personal experience with the field of gifted education when she was young, she never gave a second thought to the topic until recently, when Tina was participating in Project Synergy Preschool and was enrolled in Hollingworth Preschool. In fact, her interest and motivation were so strong that she worked on a research paper titled "A Brief Look at Gifted Education" for one of her undergraduate courses.

> Suddenly I began to feel the stresses of having a "gifted child." But this discovery was in no way negative. On the contrary, it opened up a world of new opportunities. I knew I had to learn more about the topic and I had to understand what my daughter is going through and how I could help her excel. I didn't want her to experience the negative attention I experienced when I was in school.

After "exhaustive tours, readings and reflection," Tina's mother decided to place her in a gifted program within the public school system, as opposed to a private school. The program she wanted as first schooling choice for her daughter was the Anderson Program, a self-contained program at Public School 9, on New York City's Upper West Side. Admission is based on "very superior performance on the Stanford Binet IV, school records and teacher recommendation, as well as the results of an on-site evaluation."

Despite the fact that Tina's mother "was not completely comfortable with the idea of testing children at such young ages," she pursued Anderson's application process "because there comes a time when you must place your child's best interests before your own convictions." However, a couple of weeks after taking Tina for the standardized evaluation, she learned that Tina did not score at or above the Anderson cut-off score. This meant, obviously, that the Anderson Program was no longer an option for Tina. Even though this information frustrated Tina's mother, she was still convinced that her daughter would benefit from an educational environment designed for gifted students.

Following a friend's recommendation, Tina's mother looked at the Gifted and Talented Program at Public School 163, located in community school District 3 in New York City, as an alternative to the Anderson Program. P.S. 163, as a brochure describes it, is "a good place to learn, where a multi-ethnic staff and student population work together in a nurturing learning environment." The school offers five special academic programs: An Enriched School Program (K–5), which is a basic skills program with an emphasis on problem solving, writing process and thematic teaching; a Dual Language Program (K–5), which is a full curriculum in English and Spanish; a Gifted and Talented Program (K–4), which is an enriched, individualized and differentiated curriculum for gifted students; a Dual Language Program for Gifted and Talented (K–4), which is open to both English and Spanish dominant students who have been accepted by the District to the Gifted and Talented Program, and provides an opportunity to learn in two languages concurrently; and Explorations (2–5), a program for gifted students with learning disabilities. The total school enrollment is 852 students. The admission process to the Gifted and Talented Program requires an application, a teacher evaluation, and a standardized test (no fixed cut-off scores are required).

Tina was accepted into the Gifted and Talented Program, where she began first grade. The first grade year was, in general, satisfactory. Initially, Tina had some difficulties adjusting to the new environment but experienced no significant emotional, academic, or social distress. According to her mother, "Tina's strong character helped her probably make the transition." She continues talking about her transition and adjustment to P.S. 163, saying:

> I had to understand that Tina was going to join a class where the children already knew each other because those children were coming from kindergarten, just like in Hollingworth. She joined the afternoon class where the children were together for over a year. Fortunately, she wasn't the only new student in the class; five other children joined the class that year.
>
> At the beginning Tina was reacting kind of...like her attitude was changing. I don't know if it was the new school or it was a matter of growing and developing. The teacher told me that sometimes she didn't want to participate in the classroom, she just sat there without interacting, like nothing was attractive to her.

The teacher told me not to be alarmed, that this attitude was also seen in other girls in the class, and that she is going to be OK.

I talked to Tina to see if there was something wrong, but she said everything was OK, so I took it as a period of adjustment and transition. Also, at the beginning it was a little bit difficult for her not to take part that much in the learning process. Like, everything is very established, especially coming from Hollingworth, where she was very actively involved.

Tina herself reported that she was very happy in her new school. According to her mother, Tina is very aware of the fact that she is in the Gifted and Talented program, as opposed to a regular first grade program. She knows that there is a difference between her class and the other class, because "they do things separately from the rest of the school, they go on field trips separately, they have different activities, they have their own picnics, they study differently." In other words, Tina knows and deals, apparently, very positively with the gifted label. Not only does she constantly hear about it, but also the school itself makes a definite distinction between the special classes and the regular ones.

Tina's social circle expanded as she gained more friends at her new school; she was well liked by her classmates. Academically speaking, she responded very positively and productively to the demands of the enriched and challenged gifted classroom as she continued developing her talent potential.

Tina's mother confessed to be happy seeing Tina in a place where "she can express herself, she has special needs and they are being met there so she is happy and pretty comfortable."

Although Tina's mother is relying on the school to meet Tina's academic and social needs, she is very much aware of the over-crowded conditions of the classroom and the challenging task the teacher has in meeting every child's needs. Therefore, Tina's mother is not abandoning her involvement and stimulating role in Tina's education. On the contrary, as Tina grows up, not only is she more involved and dedicated, but the messages regarding the importance of being educated are stronger and more direct.

Tina attended P.S. 163 from first to fifth grade.

"A Dual Language Program for Gifted Children? No, I Don't Think So"

The way in which Tina's mother supports and sustains Tina in her academic success is multifaceted. She demonstrates her support through involvement, high expectations, constant communication with her daughter and school, respect, and advocacy for her educational career. Interestingly enough just as Tina's mother favored and pursued her desire to place Tina in a special school for gifted children so her special needs could be addressed, she also objected to enrolling her in a bilingual program, even one designed exclusively for gifted children. A bilingual program for Tina, given that she is already bilingual and could improve and expand her language skills, was not considered to be the best decision in terms of academic achievement and performance. This conviction is founded, on the one hand, on Tina's mother's indirect but significant experience with bilingual education when she was young. On the other hand, it is based on the low performance of the children in the bilingual gifted program at P.S. 163. More specifically, Tina's mother explained during our interviews that, even though she was not placed in bilingual classes, she has friends who were placed in such classes and the differences in terms of academic development and performance were, and still are, very different:

> First of all, the way we speak the English language is very different. They have very strong accents. Also, I write much better English than they do, and I understand more English than they do. I know my friends are not comfortable enough to do their own writing. I don't feel that way. I can sit at a computer and write a ten-page paper and not think twice about the words I am using. I always say to them: are you really a great product of bilingual education?

On the other hand, when Tina's mother had the option of enrolling Tina in the Dual Language Program for Gifted and Talented children at P.S. 163, she decided not to, basically because of the academic level of performance of the children in the bilingual class, as she avidly expressed in the following excerpts:

> When I visited the school for the first time, I talked to the person who took us on the tour about the bilingual program regarding the

reading level of the children in the bilingual program in comparison
to the ones in the monolingual program. She said no, what you lose,
unfortunately, is the child is not learning in English only, so you are
not spending the same time in your efforts with English. The only
advantage, of course, is that the child picks up another language, but
Tina doesn't need the other language, and I survived on a monolingual program. I didn't feel that Tina actually needed the dual language program, especially if I knew her reading was not going to be,
you know, like a higher level. In addition, when I observed the bilingual classes I realized that, yes, the kids know both languages, but
Tina was learning about more sophisticated things.

Tina's mother does not completely oppose bilingualism, and, in
fact, during our interviews she concentrated mainly on the language component as it relates to the field of bilingual education.
She never really delved deeply into the discussion of culture as it
relates to their Hispanic background.

When Tina was a little girl, her mother wanted her to become
bilingual, so she decided to speak only Spanish at home, given
that she will get the English in school. However, she never really
pursued this decision aggressively, and in spite of the fact that
Tina can be considered somewhat bilingual, as she is able to communicate in both languages, inevitably she is becoming more and
more English dominant, with less and less Spanish vocabulary
and fluency. Tina's mother acknowledged that she tends to speak
to Tina in English most of the time, except when her grandmother
is around.

I never really pushed Tina to speak one or the other language
(Spanish or English). I never even tried to force her to use one language over the other. She uses the one who she is more comfortable
with, and most of the time it is English.

Tina's academic success cannot be overlooked. She is part of
an educational setting where her academic, social, and emotional
as well as her language and cultural needs are being met so far.

✥

Part IV

Conclusions
and Implications

Chapter Nine

Conclusions and Implications

The stories of Oscar, Gaby, and Tina are powerful examples of parental involvement, of the value of a differentiated education to meet everyone's individual needs, of a desire to do well and succeed in new and demanding academic environments, and of constant attempts to pursue the American Dream.

These young people are not meant to represent all other students from Hispanic background with superior academic potential. Each of their stories is unique. As case studies, they provide vivid portraits of the perceptions, feelings, and educational experiences of particular children and their families. They are examples of the multifaceted and heterogeneous conceptions of giftedness and its development, of the value and impact of identifying and nurturing talent potential in young children, and of the fundamental role parents play in providing their children with the best educational opportunities possible. All of these examples are embedded in the context of a multicultural society where its members are constantly fighting for identity and survival. These portraits can serve to highlight the need to promote fluent bilingualism as a cognitive advantage, and as an intellectual and cultural resource. Also, they can provide examples of the need for a comprehensive definition, identification, education, and parental advocacy in gifted bilingual populations. In sum these case studies can serve as a model for parent advocacy and educational options when dealing with the identification and education of gifted bilingual children.

Promoting Bilingualism
and Maintaining Cultural Pride

Charges of ineffectiveness have permeated bilingual education programs. The implementation of bilingual education programs has been affected by the uneven funding and interpretations provided by different political administrations. There is considerable inconsistency among the different types of programs and in the use of the same term across different typologies. At the same time, there is a proliferation of different terms for the same type of program. In addition, there is a lack of specialized programs for gifted bilingual students, even in states with high concentration of Hispanic students. None of the three parents in the case studies visited knew, or were interested in, registering their children in a bilingual gifted program. In each case, several different factors contributed to this decision.

Oscar's family looked for schools that involved challenges and rich experiences that stimulated and brought forth Oscar's capacities. His family never looked for, or intended to place him in, a bilingual program. Oscar's family's argument against a bilingual program was that since they provided at home the language and cultural experiences their children need to feel, act, and identify themselves as Hispanics, a bilingual school was unnecessary. What seems to be important here is for the children to be in a good school and be prepared for the future.

Gaby's mother admitted she would have loved to have Gaby attend a bilingual elementary school. She even regretted, at one point during the interviews, her decision to enroll Gaby in an all-English program. Gaby's mother is in favor of bilingual education, not only because she believes it is what is best for every child with a Hispanic background, but also because of Gaby's sister's positive experience with a bilingual program. However, Gaby's mother never really pursued her desire to see Gaby enrolled in a bilingual program. She was not aware of any bilingual program that would nurture their culture and language, rather than just serve as a transition to learn English.

Tina's mother objected to enrolling her in a bilingual program, even one designed exclusively for gifted children, because she questioned the effectiveness of bilingual programs. According to

Tina's mother, the academic development and level of performance of the students in the bilingual programs was much lower than that of the students in the monolingual program. For Tina's mother, it was much more important to place her daughter in an enriched, challenging, and demanding academic setting.

What Is a Bilingual Program?

Overall, the stories of the three children confirm what Cárdenas (1992) called misinformation regarding bilingual programs. He stresses that people are misinformed, or ignorant about the various types of bilingual programs, their differences, benefits, and advantages. All three mothers referred to bilingual education as a program that only provides the children with a second language, which their children already had. They ignored the benefits of learning simultaneously in two languages, of preserving the children's cultural heritage, and the definite advantage enjoyed by bilingual children in having cognitive flexibility and a diversified set of mental abilities. Oscar's and Gaby's mothers, at least, did not seem to be familiar with the different types of bilingual programs available. Their only experience was with transitional bilingual programs, which Oscar and Gaby attended when they were in kindergarten. In both cases, the mothers saw the bilingual program as strictly a remedial effort, designed to overcome the children's language deficiencies, an argument commonly found in the literature by those who oppose bilingual education.

There was general agreement among the mothers about the importance of speaking Spanish to maintain their Hispanic culture and heritage. However, Spanish was used not as part of their children's curriculum and instruction, but exclusively at home. This conception of the place of Spanish can be seen as a way for the mothers to recognize that English language competence and educational achievement are significantly and positively correlated. In fact, the scholarship literature emphasizes it. The higher the English language proficiency, the higher the academic achievement. Consequently, it can strongly be associated with higher educational aspirations, a fact that has never been in dispute in the arguments of bilingual education advocates.

It is not the intention of bilingual educators to delay the acquisition of English. The value of acquiring English and acquiring it quickly is part of the bilingual discourse. With a good bilingual program there should not be incompatibility between learning English, preserving the native language, and creating an educationally competitive and challenging program.

Bilingual education needs to be understood more deeply than simply as an issue of learning a second language. The fundamentals of bilingual education for curriculum and instruction reside in acquiring, developing, and maintaining the use of two languages. The ultimate goal is to create individuals who are biliterate. At the same time, cultural heritage is preserved and cultural pride is strengthened. Parents need to understand and to be clear on this conception when considering bilingual education for their children.

Dissemination of information regarding the availability, special characteristics, and advantages of bilingual programs—and specifically, of special programs for gifted bilingual students—needs to be considered a priority among educators. Programs need not only to accept but also to build on the students' culture and language. This practice is not, and should not, be exclusively targeted for families with dual language backgrounds. Monolingual speakers of English can and should also be included in bilingual programs. The literature available on dual bilingual programs, in which speakers of two languages are placed together in a bilingual classroom to learn each other's language and work academically in both languages, suggests that it provides a powerful incentive for both groups while developing bilingualism and positive attitudes toward diversity (Crawford, 1997; Hornberger & Micheau, 1991; Lessow-Hurley, 2000; Ovando & Collier, 1997; Pérez & Torres-Guzmán, 1996).

Defining the Term Hispanic

The term *Hispanic* should imply not just language usage but also cultural identity, a sense of belonging. Within the Spanish-speaking population there are differences in political perspective, phenotype, language dialect, culture, migration histories, language proficiency (both for Spanish and English), and modes of assimilation in the United States. Therefore, the one-size-fits-all label, whether it be Hispanic, Latino, or Chicano, deserves to be used with defined judgment.

Becoming *Hispanic-American* does not mean learning English and forgetting one's native language, or learning to eat, dress, talk, and even behave like American children. According to Rumbaut (1996), becoming American may take different forms, has different meanings, and is reached by different paths. But the process of defining an identity is one in which all children of immigrants are engaged. These children need to find a meaningful place in a society of which they are the newest members. The process is complex, conflictual, and stressful, and affects the consciousness of immigrant parents and children alike.

Growing up bilingual and bicultural is a difficult process, even under the best circumstances. Doing so in today's America is still a great challenge. For the three individuals in the case studies, this challenge is evident. The language pattern shown by the three students is to continue speaking the parental tongue (Spanish) at home but English in school. Little by little English is dominating their day and Spanish is reserved for conversations with the parents only. The three students understand and are able to communicate in Spanish but they are not moving toward being fully literate in the Spanish language. In Tina's case, for example, the usage of Spanish at home has been reduced to a minimum; she uses it only when grandma is around. Unless the families and school put an effort to promote bilingualism and biliterate, the passage of time will lead eventually toward greater English proficiency and English preference and gradual abandonment of the native language.

The Conception and Characteristics of Talent Potential in Hispanic Populations

Understanding the causes for the acknowledged underrepresentation of children from culturally and linguistically different groups, particularly Hispanics, in programs for the gifted, as well as providing the appropriate programs, have been the focus of considerable research and reflection.

Reasons for their low representation vary, often reflecting a combination of factors related to the definition and conception of giftedness adopted and the identification procedure used. The stories of the three individuals voice this reality. The value of adopting a conception of giftedness that views giftedness as a potential to be nurtured more broadly, composed of a variety of factors, more flexible, inclusive, and acknowledging language and cultural differences, increases the potential for identifying a greater number of gifted children from Hispanic background.

The stories of Oscar, Gaby, and Tina generated an emerging profile of a potentially gifted Hispanic student. This profile emerged from the description of talent or ability provided by the subjects' families, their teachers, and the students themselves. The profile is based on the following characteristics that are of a behavioral nature: (a) has potential for above-average academic achievement; (b) is a quick learner; (c) has superior memory; (d) is a productive academic worker; (e) is an avid reader; (f) exhibits superior drawing ability; (g) rapidly acquires English language skills once exposed to the language in school setting; (h) has superior verbal and communication ability in Spanish, English, or both languages; (i) is curious; (j) is alert; and (k) is a social person.

Not all potentially gifted Hispanic students will exhibit all the characteristics listed above, as was the case with Oscar, Gaby, and Tina. One cannot assume that all Hispanic students with talent potential are alike. However, these descriptors should be taken into account when identifying talent potential in bilingual students using varied forms of identification. In addition, it is very important to conceptualize giftedness in terms of potential to be realized throughout appropriate educational services, opportunities, and experiences. The confluence of personal, academic, environmental, linguistic, and cultural factors determines the presence of such potential. Based on the portraits of the three subjects and on the description of talent provided by the subjects' families, their teachers, and the students themselves, several possible indicators can be included within each of these factors as follows:

1. Personal. Aspiration, motivation, dedication, and a sense of being special are personal indicators that can be found in a student with potential for giftedness.

2. Academic. These behavioral indicators can include: (a) advanced academic performance; (b) advanced academic skills like quickness to learn, superior memory, productive work habits, avid reading interests; (c) superior drawing skills; (d) advanced communicative and language skills in Spanish, English, or both languages; (e) inquisitive and alert attitude; (f) sophisticated social skills.

3. Environmental. These factors include the presence of a family system that aspires for high educational attainment, and exhibits attitudes of advocacy, support, and involvement throughout the child's educational career.

4. Linguistic and cultural. These factors refer to the presence of a strong sense, pride and respect for the student's language and Hispanic culture.

These factors require precise assessment using varied and nontraditional measures and placement in appropriate educational services that would meet the child's needs and would foster eventual fulfillment.

Early Identification of
Potentially Gifted Hispanic Children

The literature recommends the use of multiple assessment measures to give bilingual students several opportunities to demonstrate their skills and performance potential. Varied methods of identification were used to identify Oscar, Gaby, and Tina—for instance, observations, group enrichment activities, standardized assessment measures, teacher nominations, parent recommendations, and child interviews. The validity of the identification process is well reflected in the portraits. All three children participated in Project Synergy's transitional services and summer science camp for gifted children; attended selective schools for children with superior abilities and educationally competitive programs; and received positive evaluations and comments from the teachers, their family, and themselves regarding their potential and talents.

However, even though the children benefited from this comprehensive, nontraditional approach to identify gifted bilingual children, a follow-up program designed to evaluate their school adjustment as well as their academic progress was needed, especially in Gaby's case, given her academic difficulties. Gaby's parents needed help not only facing, accepting, and dealing with Gaby's disabilities, but they also needed to be willing to receive help and trust the system again.

Being identified as a child with potential for high academic performance strongly affected the lives of these three families and their children. In Oscar's case his mother acknowledged that her life, and certainly Oscar's, would have been very different without their participation and involvement with Project Synergy. This project showed her a world she was not aware of. Project Synergy not only reinforced in Oscar's family the fact that he had potential, but it also gave the family, and especially his mother, tools and guidance for supporting and nurturing that potential. Oscar himself stressed the increased confidence he has in his own abilities as he becomes more academically successful. He has a strong sense of commitment, motivation, and a strong supportive system that surrounds him, all basic elements needed to transform talent potential into realized giftedness.

The impact of Project Synergy Preschool in Tina's life was also positive and lasting. Since Tina was identified as a student with potential for high academic achievement, she has been exposed to new, enriched, and demanding academic experiences, and she is consistently performing at high levels. Messages regarding Tina's talent, abilities, and potential are becoming stronger and more direct. Tina's educational career is moving toward transforming her potential into realized talent.

Gaby had a different experience regarding her participation in Project Synergy. Being identified as potentially gifted resulted in mixed messages and confusion and pain. At first she was identified as a student with potential for high academic achievement so she participated in the project's transitional services. Neither Gaby's mother, her teachers (both her first grade teacher at P.S. 153 and Project Synergy's teachers), or Gaby herself, noted or reported at any time that Gaby was having difficulty in academic tasks, that she was having problems understanding and communicating in English, or that she was experiencing any other sort of problem. Apparently, things were unfolding in an acceptable way. Gaby's academic performance and level of achievement during her exposure to Project Synergy's transitional services were never documented with any kind of formal assessment.

Once at the Central Park East School, Gaby was unable to meet the basic skills and curriculum demands of the school. Gaby was developing a learning disability that took the school too much time to detect and to communicate to Gaby's parents. Early identification and educational assistance were needed when Gaby was starting her elementary school. For Gaby's parents these mixed messages of a daughter with potential for high academic performance and a daughter in need of special remedial services due to severe learning difficulties were very difficult to understand, to face, and to accept. As the portrait revealed, Gaby's parents sought their own solution, hoping to see an improvement in their daughter's academic performance. It is uncertain and perplexing if indeed repeating third grade at P.S. 153 was the right thing to do, at the right place, and with the right teacher to assist Gaby meet her needs. Despite this unfortunate reality, Gaby's mother acknowledged that participating in Project Synergy was a "positive and worthwhile experience".

Several implications derive from the identification process used with these three students. The earlier the identification of potential for high academic achievement in students who are at risk of educational disadvantagedness occurs, the better the possibility for the realization of that potential if the appropriate environmental nurturance also occurs. Oscar, Gaby, and Tina were identified as early as kindergarten and preschool. The same holds true for the provision of remedial services for academic difficulties: the earlier the identification, the sooner the intervention begins. This is the premise that underlies early intervention in the special education system. In addition, the learning progress made by potentially gifted children participating in special transitional programs should be repeatedly evaluated not only in order to assess the admission decision but also to validate the decision strategy. Gaby would have benefited tremendously from such evaluation. Educational strategies for meeting her needs could have been developed, as well as a support system for her parents. Borland (1989), Callahan and Caldwell (1986), and Feldhusen and Van-Tassel-Baska (1985) have been quite insistent on including a program evaluation as an integral part of program planning and design.

Subsequently, designing and incorporating a follow-up program to evaluate the students' school adjustment is also essential, especially in cases of gifted bilingual students attending academic programs away from their familiar neighborhoods, and with different philosophies and educational approaches. Follow-up activities are not only necessary but can be highly useful in assessing the way the school is meeting the students' academic, social, emotional, cultural, and linguistic needs.

Meeting the Educational Needs
of Gifted Hispanic Children

The literature review on programming options for gifted children indicates that, once the children are identified as having high academic potential, some form of differentiated curriculum is necessary if they are to develop and nurture their potential and, eventually, transform it into realized ability. However, according to Borland (1994), the case of the children identified by Project Synergy and Project Synergy Preschool indicates that, given their lack of enrichment activities at home in some of the cases, the kind and quality of the classroom experience, and, specifically for the bilingual children, their lack of English proficiency, these children could not be placed directly in special schools or programs for gifted children because the risk of failure and maladjustment could be high, despite their potential for high academic achievement. As a consequence, the identified children were placed in a special intervention program, which consisted of transitional services, mentorship with gifted adolescents, and parent workshops. Once the intervention program was over, appropriate school placement followed.

The transitional services were successful in meeting the academic needs of Oscar and Tina, and in satisfactorily helping them make the transition to a special program for gifted children. Gaby's case, on the other hand, does not show a great deal of success from the intervention. Despite the fact that the primary focus of the transitional services was on academic skills, particularly reading, writing, and arithmetic, Gaby was unable to adjust and to function in a demanding, active, and challenging program after participating in the transitional services. Her level of achievement and special needs, while in the transitional services, needed to be closely assessed to make sure she was ready for the transition to a new and challenging environment.

Parental Reactions to Special Programs for the Gifted
Although there is no research available in the area of Hispanic parents' reaction to educational programming options for potentially gifted children, the findings speak for themselves. It should be emphasized that all three parents readily agreed to participate in the project, attended the parents workshops as part of the transitional services, brought their children during the summer and Saturday sessions consistently, and acknowledged the advantages and benefits of such opportunity.

Courage and confidence were required for Oscar's mother who, with a lack of English proficiency, not much of a knowledge base, and little experience with gifted education, managed to be informed about the program and to actively participate in the workshops and meetings. All of this was done for the sake of Oscar's education.

Like Oscar's mother, lacking experience and knowledge regarding the area of potentially gifted children, Gaby's mother understood that her daughter was among the best students in her kindergarten class and needed to be in a special program to nurture those special qualities. Lack of English proficiency and encountering a new and different world did not interfere with Gaby's mother's conviction that "if you have children and opportunities that will benefit them arise, one should take advantage of them."

Tina's mother, on the other hand, who already had identified her daughter's superior abilities and continuously received messages regarding them, participated in the project's transitional services because she knew that Tina would receive the attention that she needed. The program helped reinforce Tina's mother's perception regarding her daughter's superior abilities. She got guidance and support to deal with a child with superior abilities and help in finding a good educational program that would continue meeting Tina's academic, social, and emotional needs.

In all three cases the findings reflect the mothers' reactions as being encouraging and admirable. Their cooperation, advocacy, and determination to give their children the best educational opportunities available were sustained. All three mothers agreed that their experience with Project Synergy or Project Synergy Preschool was worth repeating.

Student Reaction to Special Programs for the Gifted
Support and correlation from the research literature on the student reaction to educational programming options for potentially gifted children is also lacking. The three portraits reveal that the students' reaction to the transitional services was positive and promising. In all three cases, the students emphasized how happy, productive, busy, and excited they were while attending the different programs of Project Synergy or Project Synergy Preschool. Everything in the transitional services was a new experience for the three students: visiting the university; the teachers of the projects; their classmates; the materials used in the classroom; the topics they studied; and especially, the great opportunity they had to be in a program where they could learn without being bored and realized they were able to process the information and respond to a challenging educational experience. All these experiences made the three students feel "special" and resulted in positive self-esteem and self-confidence. The students appreciated the educational opportunity and, even though they all wished the programs had prolonged, they seemed to be prepared to move on to other academic settings.

Mentorship Component of Special Programs for the Gifted
The idea of linking a potentially gifted young child with an older academically gifted student from the same city and the same cul-

ture promises a number of benefits. The gifted adolescent is a living example of an intelligent person who has achieved academic success. Adolescent mentors can familiarize young potentially gifted children with the activities that lead to success in their area of expertise by guiding them in the classroom. However, in the present study, the outcomes of the mentoring relationship were not immediately visible. Neither Oscar, Gaby, nor Tina at any time during our interviews commented on or referred to the mentors in great detail. The three students neither volunteered nor answered questions regarding the mentors. The three students could not even recall the mentors' names. In all three cases they only recalled having "fun" with the mentors, and they saw them as "big kids who played and spent the day with them at Synergy school." None of the three students developed a long-lasting relationship with the mentors.

Perhaps the mentors did serve both as a living example of an intelligent young person, who has achieved academic success and as a model of appropriate classroom behaviors; however, based on the findings of the present study, the long-term influence of the mentoring relationship on the academic lives of Oscar, Gaby, or Tina cannot be appraised. Either the time the mentors spent with the potentially gifted students was too short to affect their academic lives; or neither the mentors, the children, or their families understood the role the mentoring relationship was playing in the program in order to take advantage of it, encourage it, and benefit from it.

Parent Workshops in Special Programs for the Gifted
The last component of the transitional services is the parent workshops. Both Project Synergy and Project Synergy Preschool held seminars for parents concurrently with the transitional-services sessions for the children. Some of the topics discussed in the workshops were: building self-esteem in themselves and in their children, learning how to advocate for their children, becoming more knowledgeable about their children, developing positive discipline methods, involving their children in enrichment activities at home, and questions and answers regarding school-placement options for their children.

All three mothers considered the parent workshops a success. Oscar's, Gaby's, and Tina's mothers agreed on the benefits, positive impact of, and importance of the topics dealt with in the workshops. In the case of Oscar's mother, despite the fact that she was not extremely interactive during the actual seminars because of the language barrier (she had to attend the seminars in English because there were no Spanish seminars at that point in the project), she never missed a session, and she also managed to get the printed information obtained from the seminar translated into Spanish. Oscar's mother reported obtaining from the seminars many strategies and a great deal of information as to how to advocate for her son's education and how to provide optimal educational experiences and opportunities. Throughout the seminars, and in their experience with Project Synergy in general, she and her family strengthened their perception regarding Oscar as an intelligent, motivated, and committed person.

Gaby's mother attended the seminars in Spanish, giving her the advantage of participating in more interactive ways. Her attendance was also consistent. She acknowledged her participation in the workshops as beneficial and useful. She learned what educational supplies are best for her daughter, how and what type of books to read to her, how to help her with homework, and which different educational after-school activities were available for her daughter.

Tina's mother attended Project Synergy Preschool seminars and, as she stressed, they were extremely helpful and instructive. Most of all, her perception regarding Tina's talent and potential became stronger and more direct.

The constant participation and engagement of the mothers in the workshops, and in the project in general, is a clear indication that the motivation and desire existed to help their children succeed and to provide them with the best educational opportunities possible. The workshops provided them with information and skills that help them give their children the supportive background they need to succeed in their academic endeavors.

It is of critical importance to include a parent education component when dealing with the identification and education of gifted bilingual children. Hispanic parents of potentially gifted children need to be knowledgeable regarding the advantages and benefits of special programs for gifted children. In addition, they need to be involved in the school decision-making process, and they need to learn how to support and nurture their children's ability and potential. This will prevent what Bernal (1976) refers to as a passive role in the education of Hispanic children. Parents of gifted students may be concerned about messing something up with their children. They are afraid to give wrong advice and do something that might hurt their children somehow. The series of workshops empowered the three parents through the knowledge they obtained regarding their children's abilities and talent and how to advocate for their children. Their constant involvement, support and advocacy were significant in their children's educational careers.

In addition, it was important to consider language needs when communicating with the parents. If parents are not comfortable with or fully proficient in English, the communication needs to be done in their native language. This way, parents will not be discouraged to participate, and they will feel that their culture and language are respected and validated.

Parent Advocacy, Support, and Involvement

Because of the retrospective nature of the portraits, it was possible to discern patterns of behavior over a period of time and the effects this behavior had on the individuals involved. The parents in this study, especially the mothers, had to become advocates for their children in order to get the educational services they needed. They had to learn to trust and work with people from Project Synergy and Project Synergy Preschool to discover a world they were not aware of. They had to learn the workings of an educational system that was unfamiliar to them. They had to extend the learning experience to home. Providing their children with the best educational opportunities possible was the goal of these patterns of behavior.

A fundamental role the three mothers took was extending their parental involvement beyond school activities, and this role needs to be validated and supported. In other words, through several home practices the mothers demonstrated their support, in-

volvement, and advocacy. These home practices are not traditionally equated with school success because they are intangible, but
they can certainly be reflected in the students' learning and behaving. I am referring to the constant communication that exists
of high expectations in the family; trust in the children's educational endeavors, and enthusiasm for their children's school experiences, understanding, and respect. These practices need to be
considered part of the definition of parental involvement.

Schools need to reach out to Hispanic parents and develop
strategies to involve them more in school activities, at least in the
ways traditional parental involvement is defined. The research
literature insists that, when parents are in constant communication with the school and they are involved in positive ways, the
school improves, and the children do better. Schools need to communicate to Hispanic parents that they can be active participants
in their children's educational decisions. They need to feel comfortable visiting the classroom to observe a lesson, talking to the
teachers, asking questions, asking for help, suggesting ideas, volunteering in the classroom, and evaluating the instructional delivery—practices that do not happen very often among Hispanic
families. More often than not, Hispanic parents do not go to school
unless called, do not attend meetings or volunteer in school activities, and are not members of parent groups. Bermúdez (1994) reported that many parents feel uncomfortable within the school
environment because of a lack of communication, inaccessibility of
the meeting sites, lack of child care, negative past experiences
with schools, and hostility on the part of school personnel. School
personnel need to make every possible effort to provide flexible
and varied opportunities for parents to become involved. The
school's personnel can make an alien system more comprehensible.

It is remarkable then, considering the facts on the superficial
or minimum level of involvement of Hispanic parents, that all
three mothers were involved in school matters, and even though
they participated in school-related activities in differing degrees,
they all felt comfortable and undertook advocacy roles.

It bears repeating that when parents are in constant communication with the school and they are involved in positive ways the
school improves and the children do better. But how far along in

the individual's educational career does this statement maintain its validity? Is parental involvement significatively different in later stages of the educational career? How is it different? Does it have a different effect on the student's academic achievement and success? How much emphasis should educators place on encouraging and promoting parental involvement at later stages in their children's educational careers? Studies are needed to explore the role of parental involvement in late stages of their children's educational careers.

The Future Ahead

Although it is too early to determine whether the students portrayed in the case studies will reach their career goals and become successful adults, their stories would lead us to suspect that their future prospects are positive. Oscar's and Tina's profiles not only reflect children with potential for high academic achievement, a strong supportive and involved family, and positive educational experiences that are fostering their potential, but most of all, children who are motivated, dedicated, and believe in themselves. Gaby's profile reflects a student that, despite her academic difficulties, also has a supportive and involved family that will make every effort to overcome any troublesome period and help her succeed.

This book points out the myth of the gifted bilingual paradox. It is an indication that education of gifted bilingual students is more a possible achievement than an impossible dream. Those students are an integral part of the educational system requiring attention to be appropriately identified and nurtured so that their talent potential can be fully realized. These students are part of a social and cultural group, and teachers need to learn about it. Teachers need to become aware of how cultural differences may affect student learning and behaving and how to accommodate these differences in the classroom. Language diversity needs to be seen as an intellectual and cultural resource. Students can show potential for high academic achievement and yet be bilingual.

Bibliography

Aleman, S. R. (1993). *Bilingual Education Act: Background and reauthorization issues* (CRS Report for Congress). Washington, DC: Congressional Research Service. (ERIC Document Reproduction Service No. 365 163)

Anyon, J. (1981). Social class and school knowledge. *Curriculum Inquiry, 2*(1), 3–41.

Arvey, R. D. (1972). Some comments on culture fair tests. *Personnel Psychology, 25*(3), 433–448.

August, D., & Garcia, E. E. (1988). *Language minority education in the United States. Research, policy and practice.* Chicago: Charles C. Thomas.

Baldwin, A. Y. (1978). The Baldwin identification matrix. In A. Y. Baldwin, G. Gear & L. Lucito (Eds.), *Education planning for the gifted: Overcoming cultural, geographic, and socioeconomic barriers* (pp. 33–36). Reston: The Council for Exceptional Children.

Banks, J. A. (2000). The social construction of difference and the quest for educational equality. In R. S. Brandt (Ed.), *Education in a new era* (pp. 21–45). Alexandria: Association for Supervision and Curriculum Development.

Baral, D. P. (1979). Academic achievement of recent immigrants from Mexico. *Journal for the National Association for Bilingual Education, 3*(3), 1–13.

Beaty, J. J. (1998). *Observing development of the young child* (4th ed.). Columbus: Merrill.

Bempechat, J. (1990). *The role of parent involvement in children's academic achievement: A review of the literature* (Trends and Issues No. 14). New York: Teachers College, Columbia University, ERIC Clearinghouse on Urban Education.

Bergan, J. R., & Parra, E. B. (1979). Variations in IQ testing and instruction and the letter learning achievement of Anglo and bilingual Mexican-American children. *Journal of Educational Psychology, 71*(6), 819–826.

Bermúdez, A. B. (1994). *Doing our homework: How schools can engage Hispanic communities.* Washington, DC: Office of Educational Research and Improvement. (ERIC Document Reproduction Service No. 372 905)

Bermúdez, A. B., & Rakow, S. J. (1990). Analyzing teachers' perceptions of identification procedures for gifted and talented Hispanic Limited English Proficient (LEP) students at-risk. *The Journal of Educational Issues of Language Minority Students, 7,* 21–33.

Bermúdez, A. B., Rakow, S. J., Márquez, J. M., Sawyer, C., & Ryan, C. (1991). Meeting the needs of the gifted and talented Limited English Proficient student: The UHCL prototype. *National Association of Bilingual Education: Annual Conference Journal, 1990–1991,* 115–133.

Bernal, E. M. (1974). Gifted Mexican American children: An ethno-scientific perspective. *California Journal of Educational Research, 25*(5), 261–273.

———. (1976). Gifted programs for the culturally different. *National Association of Secondary School Principals (NASSP) Bulletin, 60*(398), 67–76.

———. (1978). The identification of gifted Chicano children. In

A. Y. Baldwin, G. H. Gear & L. J. Lucito (Eds.), *Education planning for the gifted: Overcoming cultural, geographic, and socioeconomic barriers.* Reston: The Council for Exceptional Children.

———. (1980). *Methods of identifying gifted minority students* (ERIC Report No. 72). Princeton: ERIC Clearinghouse, Educational Testing Service.

———. (1981a). *Special problems and procedures for identifying minority gifted children.* Paper presented at the Council for Exceptional Children. Conference on the exceptional bilingual child. New Orleans, LA. (ERIC Document Reproduction Service No. ED 203 652)

———. (1981b). *Intelligence tests on trial?* Creative Educational Enterprises. (ERIC Document Reproduction Service No. ED 249 295)

Betts, G. T. (1986). The Autonomous Learning Model for Gifted and Talented. In J. S. Renzulli (Ed.), *Systems and models for developing programs for the gifted and talented* (pp. 27–56). Mansfield Center, CT: Creative Learning Press.

Bloom, B., & Krathwohl, D. (1982). The cognitive and affective taxonomies. In C. J. Maker (Ed.), *Teaching models in education of the gifted* (pp. 17–54). Rockville, MD: Aspen.

Boehm, A. E., & Weinberg, R. A. (1997). *The classroom observer. Developing skills in early childhood settings* (3rd ed.). New York: Teachers College Press.

Borland, J. H. (1986). IQ Tests: Throwing out the bathwater, saving the baby. *Roeper Review, 8,* 163–168.

———. (1989). *Planning and implementing programs for the gifted.* New York: Teachers College Press.

———. (1994). Identifying and educating young economically disadvantaged urban children: The lessons of Project Synergy. In N. Colangelo, S. G. Assouline & D. L. Ambroson (Eds.), *Talent development: Proceedings of the second biennial Wallace conference on talent development* (pp. 151–172). Dayton: Ohio Psychology Press.

————, & Wright, L. (1994). Identifying young, potentially gifted, economically disadvantaged students. *Gifted Child Quarterly, 38*(4), 164–171.

Callahan, C. M., & Caldwell, M. S. (1986). Defensible evaluations of programs for the gifted and talented. In C. J. Maker (Ed.), *Critical issues in gifted education: Vol. 1. Defensible programs for the gifted* (pp. 277–296). Austin: Pro-Ed.

Camp, R., & Levine, D. (1991). Portfolios evolving: Background and variations in sixth- through twelfth-grade classrooms. In P. Belanoff & M. Dickson (Eds.), *Portfolios: Process and product* (pp. 194–205). Portsmouth, NH: Boynton/Cook.

Cárdenas, J. A. (1992). An educator's rationale for native-language instruction. In J. Crawford (Ed.), *Language loyalties. A source book on the official English controversy* (pp. 342–351). Chicago: University of Chicago Press.

————. (1995). Bilingual intelligence testing. *Intercultural Development Research Association (IDRA) Newsletter, 22*(1), 13–15, 21.

Carrasquillo, A. L. (1991). *Hispanic children and youth in the United States: A resource guide.* New York: Garland.

Chavez, E. L. (1982). Analysis of a Spanish translation of the Peabody Picture Vocabulary Test. *Perceptual and Motor Skills, 54*(3), 1335–1338.

Clark, B. (1997). *Growing up gifted. Developing the potential of children at home and at school* (5th ed.). Columbus: Merrill.

Clark, E. R. (1990). *The state of the art in research on teacher training models with special reference to bilingual education teachers.* Washington, DC: Office of Bilingual Education and Minority Language Affairs. (ERIC Document Reproduction Service No. 341 270)

Crawford, J. (1997). *Bilingual education: History, politics, theory, and practice* (4th ed.). Los Angeles: Bilingual Education Services.

Cummins, J. (1979). Linguistic interdependence and the educational development of bilingual children. *Review of Educational Research, 49*(2), 222–251.

———. (1981). Empirical and theoretical underpinnings of bilingual education. *Journal of Education, 163* (winter), 16–29.

———. (1984). *Bilingualism and special education: Issues in assessment and pedagogy.* Austin: Pro-Ed.

———. (1989). *Empowering minority students.* Los Angeles: California Association for Bilingual Education.

Davis-Simons, J. (1995). *The effects of parenting workshops on the attitudes and reported behaviors of parents of gifted Black and Latino primary grade students.* Unpublished doctoral dissertation, Teachers College, Columbia University, New York.

DeAvila, E. A., Struthers, J. A., & Randall, D. L. (1969). A group measure of the Piagetian concepts of conservation and egocentricity. *Canadian Journal of Behavioral Science, 1*(4), 263–272.

Delgado-Gaitán, C. (1994). *Empowerment in Carpinteria: A five-year study of family, school, and community relationships.* Center for Research on Effective Schooling for Disadvantaged Students, Baltimore, MD. Office of Educational Research and Improvement. Washington, DC. (ERIC Document Reproduction Service No. ED 375 228)

Delpit, L. (1995). *Other people's children. Cultural conflict in the classroom.* New York: New Press.

Dorhout, A. (1983). Student and teacher perceptions of preferred teacher behaviors among the academically gifted. *Gifted Child Quarterly, 27*(3), 122–125.

Dunham, G., & Russo, T. (1983). Career education for the disadvantaged gifted: Some thoughts for educators. *Roeper Review, 5,* 26–28.

Eby, J. W., & Smutny, J. F. (1990). *A thoughtful overview of gifted education.* White Plains: Longman.

Edwards, C. P., Logue, M. E., & Russell, A. J. (1983). Talking with young children about social ideas. *Young Children, 39,* 12–20.

Eliason, C., & Jenkins, L. (1994). *A practical guide to early childhood curriculum* (5th ed.). New York: Merrill.

Epstein, J. L. (1995). School/family/community partnerships. Caring for the children we share. *Phi Delta Kappan, 76*(9), 701–712.

Epstein, N. (1992). Affirmative ethnicity. In J. Crawford (Ed.), *Language loyalties. A source book on the official English controversy* (pp. 334–342). Chicago: University of Chicago Press.

Feldhusen, J. F., & Jarwan, F. A. (1993). Identification of gifted and talented youth for educational programs. In K. A. Heller, F. J. Mönks & A. H. Passow (Eds.), *International handbook of research and development of giftedness and talent* (pp. 233–251). Tarrytown, NY: Pergamon Press.

Feldhusen, J. F., & Treffinger, D. J. (1985). *Creative thinking and problem solving in gifted education.* Dubuque: Kendall/ Hunt.

Feldhusen, J. F., & VanTassel-Baska, J. (1985). Identification and assessment of the gifted and talented. In J. F. Feldhusen (Ed.), *Toward excellence in gifted education* (pp. 69–84). Denver:

Love Publishing Company.

Ferrell, B., Kress, M., & Croft, J. (1988). Teachers of gifted students. *Roeper Review, 10*(3), 136–139.

Fishman, J. A. (1971). The sociology of language: An interdisciplinary social science approach to language in society. In J. A. Fishman (Ed.), *Advances in sociology of language* (Vol. 1, pp. 258–271). The Hague: Mouton.

Fitzgerald, E. J. (1973). *The first national conference on the disadvantaged gifted.* Los Angeles: National/State Leadership Training Institute.

Ford, D. Y., & Harris, J. J. (1990). On discovering the hidden treasure of gifted and talented African-American children. *Roeper Review, 13*(1), 27–32.

Frasier, M. M. (1993). Issues, problems and programs in nurturing the disadvantaged and culturally different talented. In K. A. Heller, F. J. Mönks & A. H. Passow (Eds.), *International handbook of research and development of giftedness and talent* (pp. 685–692). Tarrytown, NY: Pergamon Press.

Fuchigami, R. Y. (1978). Summary, analysis, and future directions. In A. Y. Baldwin, G. H. Gear & L. J. Lucito (Eds.), *Education planning for the gifted: Overcoming cultural, geographic, and socioeconomic barriers.* Reston: The Council for Exceptional Children.

Gallagher, J. J. (1994). *Teaching the gifted child* (4th ed.). Boston: Allyn and Bacon.

García, E. (1992). Teachers for language minority students: Evaluating professional standards. In *Proceedings of the Second National Research Symposium on Limited English Proficient Students: Focus on Evaluation and Measurement* (pp. 383–414). Washington, DC: Office of Bilingual Education and Minority Language Affairs.

Glazer, N. (1989). *Affirmative discrimination: Ethnic inequality and public policy.* Cambridge: Harvard University Press.

Glazer, S. M., Brown, C. S., Fantauzzo, P. D., Nuget, D. H., & Searfoss, L. W. (1993). *Portfolios and beyond: Collaborative assessment in reading and writing.* Boston: Christopher-Gordon.

González, G. (1974). Language, culture, and exceptional children. *Exceptional Children, 40,* 565–570.

González, J. M. (1994). Bilingual education: A review of policy and ideologies. In R. Rodriguez, N. J. Ramos & J. A. Ruiz-Escalante (Eds.), *Compendium of readings in bilingual education. Issues and practices* (pp. 3–13). San Antonio: Texas Association for Bilingual Education.

Guilford, J. P. (1982). The structure of intellect. In C. J. Maker (Ed.), *Teaching models in education of the gifted* (pp. 87–136). Rockville, MD: Aspen.

Hadaway, T., & Marek-Schroer, C. (1992). Multidimensional assessment of the gifted minority student. *Roeper Review, 15*(2), 73–77.

Hagen, E. (1980). *Identification of the gifted.* New York: Teachers College Press.

Hanninen, G. E. (1988). A study of teacher training in gifted education. *Roeper Review, 10*(3), 139–144.

Harris, D. (1963). *Children's drawings as measures of intellectual maturity: A revision and extension of the Goodenough draw-a-man test.* New York: Harcourt Brace & World.

Hayakawa, S. I. (1992). The case of official English. In J. Crawford (Ed.), *Language loyalties. A source book on the official English controversy* (pp. 94–100). Chicago: University of Chicago Press.

Hensel, N. H. (1991). Social leadership skills in young children.

Roeper Review, 14(1), 4–6.

Hornberger, N. H., & Micheau, C. (1991). Extending enrichment bilingual education: Revisiting typologies and redirecting policy. In O. García (Ed.), *Bilingual education: Focusschrift in honor of Joshua A. Fishman: Vol. 1. Focus on bilingual education* (pp. 215–234). Philadelphia: John Benjamins.

Inger, M. (1992). *Increasing the school involvement of Hispanic parents* (Digest No. 80). New York: Teachers College, Columbia University, ERIC Clearinghouse on Urban Education.

Jiménez, M. (1992). The educational rights of language-minority children. In J. Crawford (Ed.), *Language loyalties. A source book on the official English controversy* (pp. 243–251). Chicago: University of Chicago Press.

Kaufman, A. S., & Harrison, P. L. (1986). Intelligence tests and gifted assessment: What are the positives? *Roeper Review, 8*(3), 154–159.

Kaufman, A. S., & Kaufman, N. L. (1983). *Kaufman Assessment Battery for Children. Interpretive manual.* Circle Pines, MN: American Guidance Services.

Kingore, B. (1995). Introducing parents to portfolio assessment: A collaborative effort toward authentic assessment. *Gifted Child Today Magazine, 18*(4), 12–13, 40.

Kitano, M. (1982). Young gifted children: Strategies for preschool teachers. *Young Children, 37*(4), 14–24.

Kitano, M., & Kirby, D. F. (1986). *Gifted education. A comprehensive view.* Boston: Little Brown.

Knight, M. E., & Gallaro, D. (1994). *Portfolio assessment. Applications of portfolio analysis.* Lanham, MD: University Press of America.

Kogan-Frenk, E. (1997). *Gifted bilingual students: A paradox? Educational experiences of three gifted bilingual students.* Unpublished doctoral dissertation, Teachers College, Columbia University, New York.

Kohlberg, L. (1982). Discussions of moral dilemmas. In C. J. Maker (Ed.), *Teaching models in education of the gifted* (pp. 137–176). Rockville, MD: Aspen.

Lamb, R. A., & Busse, C. A. (1983). Leadership beyond lip service. *Roeper Review, 5*(3), 21–23.

Lambert, W. E., & Tucker, G. R. (1972). *Bilingual education of children: The St. Lambert experiment.* Rowley, MA: Newbury House.

Lareau, A. (1987). Social class differences in family-school relationships: The importance of cultural capital. *Sociology of Education, 60,* 73–85.

Lessow-Hurley, J. (2000). *The foundations of dual language instruction* (3rd ed.). White Plains: Longman.

Maddux, C. D., Samples-Lachman, I., & Cummings, R. E. (1985). Preferences of gifted students for selected teacher characteristics. *Gifted Child Quarterly, 29*(4), 160–163.

Madrid, A. (1990). Official English: A false policy issue. *Annals of the American Academy of Political and Social Science, 508,* 62–65.

Maker, C. J. (1982). *Teaching models in education of the gifted.* Rockville, MD: Aspen.

———. (1983). Quality education for gifted minority students. *Journal for the Education of the Gifted, 6*(3), 140–153.

———, & Schiever, S. W. (1989). Summary of Hispanic section. In C. J. Maker & S. W. Schiever (Eds.), *Critical issues in gifted education: Vol. 2. Defensible programs for cultural and ethnic minorities* (pp. 69–74). Austin: Pro-Ed.

Márquez, J. A., & Sawyer, C. B. (1994). *Curriculum extension for the gifted and talented students with limited English proficiency.* (ERIC Document Reproduction Service No. ED 372 642)

McLaughlin, M. W., & Shields, P. M. (1987). Involving low-income parents in the schools: A role for policy? *Phi Delta Kappan, 69*(2), 156–160.

Meeker, M., & Meeker, R. (1986). The SOI system for gifted education. In J. S. Renzulli (Ed.), *Systems and models for developing programs for the gifted and talented* (pp. 194–215). Mansfield Center, CT: Creative Learning Press.

Melesky, T. J. (1985). Identifying and providing for the Hispanic gifted child. *Journal for the National Association for Bilingual Education, 9*(3), 43–56.

Mercer, J. R. (1976). Pluralistic diagnosis in the evaluation of Black and Chicano children: A procedure for taking sociocultural variables into account in clinical assessment. In C. A. Hernández, M. J. Haug & N. N. Wagner (Eds.), *Chicanos, social and psychological perspectives* (2nd ed.) (pp. 183–195). St. Louis: Mosby.

——, & Lewis, J. F. (1978). Using the System of Multicultural Pluralistic Assessment (SOMPA) to identify the gifted minority child. In A. Y. Baldwin, G. H. Gear & L. J. Lucito (Eds.), *Education planning for the gifted: Overcoming cultural, geographic, and socioeconomic barriers* (pp. 37–40). Reston: Council for Exceptional Children.

Merriam, S. B. (1988). *Case study research in education. A qualitative approach.* San Francisco: Jossey-Bass.

Meyers, E. (1984). A study of concerns of classroom teachers regarding a resource room program for the gifted. *Roeper Review, 7,* 32–36.

Middlebrooks, M. W., & Strong, J. H. (1982). Project Career. *Roeper Review, 5,* 36–38.

Myers, B., & Goldstein, D. (1979). Cognitive development in bilingual and monolingual lower-class children. *Psychology in the Schools, 16,* 137–142.

Nazzaro, J., & Portuondo, M. (1981). Understanding where the students are coming from. In J. Nazzaro (Ed.), *Culturally diverse exceptional children in school* (pp. 1–12). Reston: Council for Exceptional Children.

Ogbu, J. U. (1986). The consequences of the American caste system. In N. Neisser (Ed.), *The school achievement of minority children: New perspectives.* Hillsdale, NJ: Erlbaum.

———. (1987). Variability in minority school performance: A problem in search of an explanation. *Anthropology and Education Quarterly, 18*(4), 312–334.

———. (1990). Minority status and literacy in comparative perspective. *Journal of the American Academy of Arts and Science, 119*(2), 141–168.

Ortiz, V., & Volloff, W. (1987). Identification of gifted and accelerated Hispanic students. *Journal for the Education of the Gifted, 11*(1), 45–55.

Ovando, C. J., & Collier, U. P. (1997). *Bilingual and English as a Second Language classrooms: Teaching in multicultural contexts* (2nd ed.). New York: McGraw Hill.

Palmer, M., & Graffney, P. D. (1972). Effects of administration of the Wechsler Intelligence Scale for Children in Spanish and English and relationship to social class and to performance. *Psychology in the Schools, 9,* 61–64.

Passow, A. H. (1980). Enrichment of education for the gifted. In A. H. Passow (Ed.), *Education for gifted children and youth: An old issue—a new challenge* (pp. 23–40). Ventura, CA: Office of the Ventura County Superintendent of school for the National/State Leadership Training Institute on the Gifted and Talented.

————. (1982). *Differentiated curricula for the gifted/talented. A point of view.* Paper presented at the meeting of the National/State Leadership Training Institute on the Gifted and Talented, Ventura, CA.

Peal, E., & Lambert, W. E. (1962). The relation of bilingualism to intelligence. *Psychological monographs: General and Applied, 76*(546), 1–23.

Pegnato, C. W., & Birch, J. W. (1959). Locating gifted children in junior high school: A comparison of methods. *Exceptional Children, 25,* 300–304.

Pérez, B., & Torres-Guzmán, M. E. (1996). *Learning in two worlds. An integrated Spanish/English biliteracy approach* (2nd ed.). White Plains: Longman.

Persell, C. H. (1977). *Education and inequality: The roots and results of stratification in America's schools.* New York: Free Press.

Portes, A. & Schauffler, R. (1996). Language and the second generation: Bilingualism yesterday and today. In A. Portes (Ed.), *The new second generation* (pp. 8–29). New York: Russell Sage.

Raven, J. (1965). *Raven's progressive matrices test.* London: Lewis.

Renzulli, J. S. (1977). *The enrichment triad model: A guide for developing defensible programs for the gifted and talented.* Mansfield Center, CT: Creative Learning Press.

Renzulli, J. S. (1984). Evaluating programs for the gifted: Four questions about the larger issues. *Gifted Education International, 2*(2), 83–87.

Renzulli, J. S., & Hartman, R. K. (1971). Scale for rating the behavioral characteristics of superior students. *Exceptional children, 38*, 243–248.

Renzulli, J. S., & Reiss, S. M. (1986). The enrichment triad/revolving door model: A schoolwide plan for the development of creative productivity. In J. S. Renzulli (Ed.), *Systems and models for developing programs for the gifted and talented* (pp. 216–266). Mansfield Center, CT: Creative Learning Press.

Renzulli, J. S., Reiss, S. M., & Smith, L. H. (1981). *The revolving door identification model.* Mansfield Center, CT: Creative Learning Press.

Renzulli, J. S., Smith, L. H., White, A. J., Callahan, C., & Hartman, R. K. (1976). *Scales for rating the behavioral characteristics of superior students.* Mansfield Center, CT: Creative Learning Press.

Resources for Youth. (1980). National Commission on Resources for Youth. In D.V. Jackson (Ed.), *Readings in curriculum development for the gifted* (pp. 175–180). Hartford: Special Learning Corporation.

Richert, E. S. (1991). Rampant problems and promising practices in identification. In N. Colangelo & G. A. Davis (Eds.), *Handbook of gifted education* (pp. 81–96). Boston: Allyn and Bacon.

Robinson, N. M., & Chamrad, D. L. (1986). Appropriate uses of intelligence tests with gifted children. *Roeper Review, 8*, 160–163.

Robisheaux, J. A., & Banbury, M. M. (1994). Students who don't fit the mold. *Gifted Child Today, 17*(5), 28–31.

Rumbaut, R. G. (1996). The crucible within: Ethnic identity, self-esteem, and segmented assimilation among children of immigrants. In A. Portes (Ed.), *The new second generation* (pp. 119–170). New York: Russell Sage Foundation.

Sattler, J. M. (1992). *Assessment of children* (3rd ed.). San Diego: Jerome M. Sattler.

Sattler, J. M., & Altes, L. M. (1984). Performance of bilingual and monolingual Hispanic children on the Peabody Picture Vocabulary Test Revised and the McCarthy Perceptual Performance Scale. *Psychology in the Schools, 21*(3), 313–316.

Schack, G. D., & Starko, A. J. (1990). Identification of gifted students: An analysis of criteria preferred by preservice teachers, classroom teachers, and teachers of the gifted. *Journal for the Education of the Gifted, 13*(4), 346–363.

Schulkind, C. R. (1982). Creative programming for the multilingual, culturally-conflicted gifted. In *Selected procedings from the fifth National conference on disadvantaged gifted/talented. Identifying and educating the disadvantaged gifted/talented* (pp. 29–37). Ventura, CA: Ventura County Superintendent of Schools Office.

Scott, M. S., Perou, R., Urbano, R., Hogan, A., & Gold, S. (1992). The identification of giftedness: A comparison of White, Hispanic, and Black families. *Gifted Child Quarterly, 36*(3), 131–139.

Shore, B. M., & Kaizer, C. (1989). The training of teachers for gifted pupils. *Canadian Journal of Education, 14*(1), 74–87.

Sternberg, R. J. (1986). Identifying the gifted through IQ: Why a little bit of knowledge is a dangerous thing. *Roeper Review, 8,* 143–147.

———, & Davidson, J. E. (1986). *Conceptions of giftedness.* Cambridge: Cambridge University Press.

Story, C. M. (1985). Facilitator of learning: A micro-ethnographic study of the teacher of the gifted. *Gifted Child Quarterly, 29*(4), 155–159.

Suárez-Orozco, M. M. (1987). Towards a psychosocial understanding of Hispanic adaptation to American schooling. In H. T. Trueba (Ed.), *Success or failure?: Learning and the language minority student* (pp. 156–168). Boston: Newbury House.

Taba, H. (1982). Teaching strategies program. In C. J. Maker (Ed.), *Teaching models in education of the gifted* (pp. 237–292). Rockville, MD: Aspen.

———, & Elkins, D. (1968). *Teaching strategies for the culturally disadvantaged.* Chicago: Rand McNally.

Tannenbaum, A. J. (1983). *Gifted children. Psychological and educational perspectives.* New York: Macmillan.

Terman, L. M. (1926). *Genetic studies of genius: Vol. 1.* Palo Alto: Stanford University Press.

Thorndike, R. L., & Hagen, E. P. (1986). *Measurement and evaluation in psychology and education.* New York: Macmillan.

Torrance, E. P. (1974). *The Torrance test of creative thinking: Technical-norms manual.* Chicago: Scholastic Testing Services.

———. (1977). *Discovery and nurturance of giftedness in the culturally different.* Reston: Council for Exceptional Children.

Tuttle, F. B., & Becker, L. A. (1980). *Characteristics and identification of gifted and talented students.* Washington, DC: National Education Association.

Udall, A. J. (1989). Curriculum for gifted Hispanic students. In C. J. Maker & S. W. Schiever (Eds.), *Critical issues in gifted* education: Vol. 2. Defensible programs for cultural and ethnic minorities* (pp. 41–56). Austin: Pro-Ed.

U.S. Bureau of the Census. (1997). *Projections of the population, by sex, race, and Hispanic origin, for regions, divisions, and states: 1995–2025* (Preferred series–PPL–47). Washington, DC: Government Printing Office.

U.S. English. (1999). States with official English laws [On-line]. Available: http://us-english.org

Valencia, A. A. (1985). Curricular perspectives for gifted Limited English Proficient students. *National Association for Bilingual Education Journal, 10*(1), 65–77.

Valverde, S. A. (1987). A comparative study of Hispanic high school dropouts and graduates: Why do some leave school early and some finish? *Education and Urban Society, 19*(3), 320–329.

VanTassel-Baska, J. (1989). Appropriate curriculum for gifted learners. *Educational Leadership*, March, 13–15.

VanTassel-Baska, J., Patton, J., & Prillaman, D. (1989). Disadvantaged gifted learners at-risk for educational attention. *Focus on Exceptional Children, 22*(3), 1–15.

Wechsler, D. (1974). *Wechsler intelligence scale for children revised.* New York: Psychological Corporation.

Weiss, P., & Gallagher, J. (1986). Project TARGET: A needs assessment approach to gifted education inservice. *Gifted Child Quarterly, 30*(3), 114–118.

Williams, F. E. (1982). Teaching strategies for thinking and feeling. In C. J. Maker (Ed.), *Teaching models in education of the gifted* (pp. 371–412). Rockville, MD: Aspen.

Willings, D. (1983). Training for leadership. Group roles and the gifted child. *Roeper Review, 5*(3), 18–21.

Woodcock, R. W., Johnson, M. B., Mather, N., McGrew, K. S., & Werder, J. K. (1977). *Woodcock-Johnson Psychoeducational Battery Revised*. New York: Riverside Publishing Company.

Woods, S. B., & Achey, V. H. (1990). Successful identification of gifted racial/ethnic group students without changing classification requirements. *Roeper Review, 13*(1), 21–26.

Wright, L., & Borland, J. H. (1992). A special friend: Adolescent mentors for young, economically disadvantaged, potentially gifted students. *Roeper Review, 14,*124–129.

————. (1993). Using portfolios in the identification of young, economically disadvantaged, potentially gifted students. *Roeper Review, 15,* 205–210.

Wright, L., & Coulianos, C. (1991). A model program for precocious children: Hollingworth Preschool. *Gifted Child Today, 15*(5), 24–29.

Zappia, I. A. (1989). Identification of gifted Hispanic students: A multidimensional view. In C. J. Maker & S. W. Schiever (Eds.), *Critical issues in gifted education: Vol. 2. Defensible programs for cultural and ethnic minorities* (pp. 19–26). Austin: Pro-Ed.

RETHINKING CHILDHOOD

JOE L. KINCHELOE & JANICE A. JIPSON, *General Editors*

A revolution is occurring regarding the study of childhood. Traditional notions of child development are under attack, as are the methods by which children are studied. At the same time, the nature of childhood itself is changing as children gain access to information once reserved for adults only. Technological innovations, media, and electronic information have narrowed the distinction between adults and children, forcing educators to rethink the world of schooling in this new context.

This series of textbooks and monographs encourages scholarship in all of these areas, eliciting critical investigations in developmental psychology, early childhood education, multicultural education, and cultural studies of childhood.

Proposals and manuscripts may be sent to the general editors:

> Joe L. Kincheloe
> 637 W. Foster Avenue
> State College, PA 16801
>
> *or*
>
> Janice A. Jipson
> 219 Pease Court
> Janesville, WI 53545

To order other books in this series, please contact our Customer Service Department at:

> (800) 770-LANG (within the U.S.)
> (212) 647-7706 (outside the U.S.)
> (212) 647-7707 FAX

Or browse online by series at:
> www.peterlangusa.com